Ask and it will be given to you; seek
and you find; knock and the door
will be opened to you.

—*Matthew 7:7 (NIV)*

MYSTERIES *of* BLACKBERRY VALLEY

Where There's Smoke

MYSTERIES *of* BLACKBERRY VALLEY

Where There's Smoke

LAURA BRADFORD

Guideposts

A Gift from Guideposts

Thank you for your purchase! We want to express our gratitude for your support with a special gift just for you.

Dive into *Spirit Lifters*, a complimentary e-book that will fortify your faith, offering solace during challenging moments. Its 31 carefully selected scripture verses will soothe and uplift your soul.

Please use the QR code or go to **guideposts.org/ spiritlifters** to download.

Mysteries of Blackberry Valley is a trademark of Guideposts.

Published by Guideposts
100 Reserve Road, Suite E200
Danbury, CT 06810
Guideposts.org

Copyright © 2025 by Guideposts. All rights reserved. This book, or parts thereof, may not be reproduced, stored in a retrieval system, or transmitted in any form or by any means, electronic, mechanical, photocopying, recording, or otherwise, without the written permission of the publisher.

This is a work of fiction. Apart from actual historical people and events that may figure into the fiction narrative, all other names, characters, businesses, and events are the creation of the author's imagination and any resemblance to actual persons, living or dead, or events is coincidental. Every attempt has been made to credit the sources of copyrighted material used in this book. If any such acknowledgment has been inadvertently omitted or miscredited, receipt of such information would be appreciated.

Scripture references are from the following sources: *The Holy Bible, King James Version* (KJV). *The Holy Bible, New International Version* (NIV). Copyright © 1973, 1978, 1984, 2011 by Biblica, Inc. Used by permission of Zondervan. All rights reserved worldwide. www.zondervan.com.

Cover and interior design by Müllerhaus
Cover illustration by Bob Kayganich at Illustration Online LLC.
Typeset by Aptara, Inc.

ISBN 978-1-961441-55-2 (hardcover)
ISBN 978-1-961441-56-9 (softcover)
ISBN 978-1-961441-57-6 (epub)

Printed and bound in the United States of America
10 9 8 7 6 5 4 3 2 1

Where There's Smoke

Chapter One

"Earth to Hannah. Come in, Hannah."

Startled, Hannah Prentiss set down the cleaning cloth and raised her head to find her best friend, Lacy Minyard, watching her closely. "I'm sorry. Did I miss something?"

Lacy nodded to the long folding table erected in the middle of the yard. "Nope. Everything looks absolutely amazing. The sandwiches. The salad. Your special peach lemonade, and those *cookies*! Are you trying to fatten us all up?"

Hannah gestured toward the hustle and bustle that was their church group. "Everyone is working so hard to get this place cleaned up for Miriam that it only seemed right to give them a proper thank-you meal. It's easy enough when you own a restaurant."

Closing the gap between them with two long strides, Lacy commandeered the cloth from Hannah's hand. "Hold still. You've got a smudge of soot on your cheek." She gave it a quick rub. "And now you don't."

"Thanks."

"Of course. I suspect you'll do the same for me at some point before we call it quits for the day."

Hannah took the cloth from Lacy and tossed it into the bag at her feet. "Every time I walk through Miriam's front door, I praise God that she was at her son's place in Cave City when the fire broke out. If she hadn't been…" She stopped, drew in a breath, and held up her hands. "Miriam is fine. That's all that matters. And the house—well, we're making progress, right?"

"We are." Lacy hooked her thumb in the direction of the yard. "Are we ready to call everyone to the table?"

Hannah took a mental inventory of every place setting, every food platter, every waiting cup. When she was satisfied all was ready, she nodded to her friend.

Soon, after hands were washed and a blessing shared over the meal, a dozen members of their church women's group pulled folding chairs up to the table and began to eat, the exhaustion from the morning's work blanketing them in a rare silence. Occasionally, a pocket of conversation sprang up, but it didn't last long against the pull of the food as they worked to refuel their bodies.

"Hannah, this salad is amazing," said Connie Sanchez, the church secretary.

The round of nodding that accompanied Connie's words continued as Vera Bowman commented on the deliciousness of the sandwiches.

"If you haven't found your way to Hannah's restaurant yet, I can assure you that this"—Lacy motioned to the food around them—"is just a preview of what the Hot Spot has to offer."

More nods made their way around the table until Vera cleared her throat and took the conversational baton again. "I have to say, I was a little skeptical about a restaurant coming into the old firehouse, but you made it work, Hannah," she said. "My kids love your food, and I like knowing they're eating things that were grown and raised in and around Blackberry Valley."

"Thank you."

"I imagine you've had quite a lot of culture shock though," Connie said, eyeing Hannah across the top of her lemonade.

Hannah set her cup down. "You mean after working in Los Angeles?" At Connie's answering nod, she continued. "I mean, sure, LA and Blackberry Valley are very, *very* different. And the restaurants I worked in there were more high-end than the Hot Spot is, but high-end doesn't mean better, and I wanted to come home. To Blackberry Valley."

"And I'm so glad you did," Lacy said, resting her hand on Hannah's and giving it a squeeze. "Having you back in Kentucky these last few months has been such a blessing."

"For me too." Returning her friend's smile, Hannah pushed away from the table. "God led me home at exactly the right time."

The sound of tires against gravel drew her attention to the driveway and the navy blue sedan slowly making its way toward the one-story home. A glance into the passenger seat showed the reason they were all there.

"Miriam's here," Hannah said. She, Lacy, and a handful of others rose to their feet. "I was hoping we'd have everything done before she came."

"Miriam Spencer may be lovable, but she's also as stubborn as the day is long," Connie said. "She's no more capable of staying away than her son is of telling her no."

It was hard not to smile at the accuracy of Connie's words. It was even harder not to smile when Miriam opened the door and got out before her son could make his way around the car.

"Goodness, how long have you all been here?" Miriam asked, her sharp gaze darting from the women walking toward her, to the table, and then to her beloved home of nearly sixty years.

Connie stepped forward. "We got here shortly after sunrise."

"Sunrise?" Miriam shot an accusatory glare at her son, Tom. "Why didn't you wake me and bring me over sooner?"

"Because you need your sleep." Hannah sidled up beside the eighty-five-year-old and planted a kiss on her wrinkled cheek. "And we wanted to surprise you by getting everything cleaned up before you returned."

Leaning against the open car door, Miriam pointed the end of her cane first at the house and then the women. "It's *my* house that caught on fire."

"Yes, but Ecclesiastes chapter four, verse nine, says two are better than one because together they can work more effectively," Hannah reminded her. She gestured at the women assembled around them. "So we came, twelve strong. We plan to get right back to work after lunch."

Miriam lowered her chin and eyed Hannah over the top of her glasses. "And who's running your new restaurant while you're here?"

"I closed for the day."

"You closed a new restaurant for an entire day?" Miriam repeated, drawing back.

"Yes, but that's okay. Tuesdays tend to be slow anyway."

"And your staff is okay missing a day's pay?"

"I'm still paying them."

"You haven't been open long enough to be giving paid days off," Miriam scolded.

"It's one day, and I'll make it work. Being here, doing this, is more important. Truly."

Rolling her eyes, Miriam turned her attention to Connie. "And who's at the church office right now?"

Connie patted her pocket. "I've forwarded all calls to my cell."

"And you?" Miriam shifted her focus to Lacy. "Who's looking after those chickens of yours?"

Lacy swapped grins with Hannah. "My chickens are fine, Miriam."

"We *want* to be here," Vera said, and the others echoed agreement. "To help get you back into your house."

"Helping me is fine. Doing it without me isn't." Miriam planted the end of her cane on the ground and shoved her car door closed. "So let's get to it, shall we?"

The group made its way to the house, stopping en route to pick up the cleaning supplies and brooms they'd left beside the front door at lunchtime. Connie and her group of five broke right toward the kitchen, Vera and her helpers made a beeline for the primary bedroom, and Hannah and Lacy led Miriam and Tom into the living room.

"We've made a lot of headway on the smell in here, and we've pulled up the floorboards closest to the fireplace, as you can see." Hannah crossed the remaining scorched floorboards and retrieved the pry bar she'd left in the corner. "If we can get the rest of these up by the end of the day, the men can come and put in a new floor on Saturday."

Miriam gazed around the room, tsking softly beneath her breath.

"It's all fixable," Hannah said soothingly. "Even the guest room with all of its damage. Really. And you're safe and sound. That's all that matters."

"That's what I keep telling her," Tom chimed in.

"I don't know if I have the strength to pull up floorboards," Miriam murmured.

"You don't have to. Lacy and I have this covered. Right, Lacy?"

"Right." Lacy pointed at the stack of books they'd made that morning. "But if you could inspect those and rid them of any soot, Miriam, that would be helpful."

Miriam's gaze skirted to the books. "I can do that."

"Perfect."

When the elderly woman was settled in a folding chair on the other side of the room, Hannah, Lacy, and Tom got to the business of pulling up the rest of the floor. Board by board, they made their way from the fireplace to the center of the room, setting some aside and discarding others out in the yard.

It was slow, tedious work as they stood, crouched, and stood, again and again as the June sun made its way across the sky, trading the noon hour for the afternoon, and then the afternoon for the early evening.

Rolling her shoulders in an attempt to work out a growing kink, Hannah took a moment to survey what was left and weigh it against the chores she knew still faced Lacy at her farm. An hour's work, maybe, if they continued the course. Two hours if she took over from this point by herself.

"Lacy?"

Her friend wiped a bead of sweat from her face. "What's up?"

"Go home. I'll take it from here."

"I can't do that," Lacy protested.

"You still have farm chores to take care of. Go."

Lacy pulled her phone from her pocket and consulted the screen. "Are you sure? Because I could do those and come right back."

"I've got it. Really."

Lacy put her pry bar down and stood. "I'll clean up from lunch before I leave."

"Vera already took care of that," Tom said from the corner of the room where he was working.

"See?" Hannah waved toward the door. "All that's left are the horses."

"The horses and that corner of the room," Lacy said, pointing at the section behind Hannah.

"I've got it," Hannah repeated, smiling. "We can finish up."

In an effort to prove her words, Hannah crouched down, worked to hook the pry bar between the board she'd most recently dislodged and the loose one beside it, and pulled. Her gaze fell on a small wooden compartment cast in shadows. "Whoa. What's this?" she said as she leaned closer.

"What's what?" Lacy and Tom asked in unison.

She reached inside and ran her fingers along the intact wooden box. "It looks like a hiding place of some kind."

The thump of Miriam's cane was followed by her voice on the other side of Hannah. "A hiding place?"

"Yes, look." Pointing to the box, Hannah glanced at her elderly friend. "You don't know about this?"

"No. And I've lived here for nearly sixty years. Tom?"

"I had no idea."

Hannah handed him the pry bar and addressed Miriam again. "The lid isn't on right—it's crooked. Do you want me to look inside?"

"I think you'd better."

Hannah pushed aside the compartment's lid and reached inside the dusty box, her fingertips grazing paper before landing on something round and hard and—

She closed her hand around the object and drew it out. When the object was revealed, they all gasped.

"Whoa," Hannah murmured at the sight of an exquisite ruby brooch, its large gem sparkling in the early evening rays slanting in from the open window.

"It's magnificent," Miriam said in a raspy voice.

Tom squatted beside Hannah. "I don't understand. How could something like this be hidden under a floorboard in a house my mom has owned for longer than I've been alive—yet none of us knew it was here?"

Hannah heard the question, even registered it on some level, but her focus was on the brooch. A brooch that sparkled in the sun.

"I don't know how I *couldn't* know," Miriam said, shaking her head. "It's my house. Before now, I would have said I knew everything about this place."

"You never had a reason to pull up the floor, Mom," Tom pointed out.

Hannah looked from the polished jewel in her hand to the dusty box in which it had been hidden, her gaze landing on the other item she'd felt. Tom reached inside and pulled it out. "Is that a flyer of some kind?" she asked.

"I think so." Holding it to the side, he blew dust off the paper. "Put there as a cushion to protect the brooch, I'd guess."

Hannah watched Tom carefully smooth out the page to reveal an advertisement for what appeared to be classic cars and then returned her full attention to the ruby brooch as she rose to her feet. "I wonder how long this has been here."

"Based on the dust and the fact that Mom's lived here for almost sixty years, I'd say a long time." Tom balled up the flyer and tossed it in a nearby trash can. "A *very* long time."

"If you're right, and this was here before Miriam moved in, someone has come back to it since," Hannah said.

Miriam eyed Hannah. "How can you know that, dear?"

Hannah held out her hand and opened her fingers to reveal the brooch. "Look at it. Look at the way it shines."

Miriam gasped again. "You're right. It's been freshly polished!"

Chapter Two

"Good morning, Hot Spot team! Did you enjoy your unexpected day off yesterday? Because mine was something to write home about, that's for sure." Hannah breezed through the swinging doors into the kitchen of her restaurant. And then she saw the woebegone expressions of her staff.

Raquel Holden, a usually bubbly and oh-so-adept waitress, quickly shifted her apron-clad body in front of a prep-space counter and stared at the freshly mopped linoleum floor beneath her feet.

Hannah's young waiter, Dylan Bowman, ran his fingers through his wavy red hair and cleared his throat nervously as he looked at everyone and everything around them except Hannah.

And Hannah could feel the tension emanating from her head chef, Jacob Forrest, as if it were a living, breathing thing.

"What?" Hannah asked against the backdrop of the doors whooshing closed behind her. "What did I miss?"

Jacob snatched a copy of the *Blackberry Valley Chronicle* from the counter behind Raquel and gave it a shake. "Based on the smile you were wearing a second ago, I'd say you missed *this*."

"Oh. Right. The review on the Hot Spot is supposed to be out today." Stepping forward, Hannah reached for the paper but then paused. "Uh-oh. It's not good, is it?"

Raquel's attempt at a smile was fast, fleeting.

Dylan poked at a nonexistent spot on the floor with the toe of one high-top sneaker.

Jacob shook the paper once more before drawing it close enough to read aloud. "'Housed in the original Blackberry Valley fire station, the Hot Spot isn't quite what I wanted it to be. Was it fun to be seated at a table near the pole that so many firemen slid down to go fight a fire? Sure. But other than the presence of the pole and the garage-size dining area, the firehouse feel was rather lackluster.'"

"Having a coiled water hose attached to the back wall doesn't say *firehouse* to him?" Hannah protested. "Or the glass case with the fire axes we have hanging in the entryway?"

Jacob glared at the paper. "According to Marshall Fredericks, our local food critic, that may say *firehouse* in the most basic of ways, but it doesn't say *Blackberry Valley* firehouse."

"How exactly would we say that?"

"There's more." He continued reading. "'In fact, the theme felt generic, like one might find in a chain restaurant anywhere in America. I wanted more from the Hot Spot.'"

"*Generic?*" Hannah echoed. "Really?"

"May I?" Jacob's left eyebrow arched as he glanced back up at Hannah.

Clenching her jaw, she nodded.

"'The waiter who took my order was pleasant enough, but I nearly wore my soda in his haste to set it in front of me, and he didn't leave me enough time to properly enjoy my salad before bringing my dinner order to the table.'"

Dylan's cheeks were bright red, and his narrow shoulders slouched. "I'm sorry, Hannah. I get ahead of myself sometimes. I'm working on it."

"I know you are, Dylan, and that's all I can ask," Hannah said. "Timing is a tricky thing to learn in a restaurant, but you'll get it."

Jacob cleared his throat and returned to the review. "'While the farm-to-table menu contained a sprinkling of some cleverly named selections, the descriptions didn't match the surroundings or the customer base in all cases.'"

She felt the weight of Raquel's knowing gaze and did her best to remain focused on her head chef as he hastily moved on.

"'And then there's the food.'" Jacob stopped reading for a moment, drew in a breath, and then released it in a single, irritated huff. "'I ordered the Five Alarm Burger, drawn in by both the clever name and my affinity for innovative combinations—in this case, cream cheese, fried jalapenos, and raspberry-pepper jelly. The burger was good, and the spicy flavor combination intriguing, but if the promised raspberry-pepper jelly had been used *on* the burger rather than as a drawing tool *around* it, it might have actually measured up to its name.'"

Hannah drew back. "Jacob, tell me you didn't."

"It was our latest menu addition, and I wanted it to be memorable. Besides, I do put the jelly on the burger. What I add to the plate is simply decorative."

"Well, it was certainly memorable for Marshall Fredricks," Hannah managed to say past the growing lump in her throat. "Now we have to hope it's not quite so memorable for the people whose first introduction to the Hot Spot comes from that review."

Raquel made her way over to Hannah, her trademark smile and happy-go-lucky personality back on full display. "Marshall Fredricks is one person, Hannah. *One*."

"One person whose words are read by just about everyone in Blackberry Valley," Jacob muttered.

"Maybe he'll give us another chance," Dylan suggested.

Hannah and Jacob exchanged knowing looks. "It doesn't usually work that way, Dylan," Hannah said. "Not in the restaurant business anyway."

"I'm sorry, Hannah," Jacob said gruffly. "I know I tend to go a little overboard sometimes."

"No. It's my restaurant, and clearly, I need to do better," Hannah said.

Jacob wadded up the paper and tossed it in the recycling bin. "We all do. And we will. You have my word on that."

Hannah plucked the paper out again and extracted the section with the review.

"What are you doing?" Jacob asked. "We don't want that."

"Maybe we don't want it, but we absolutely *need* it. *I* need it."

Raquel stepped up beside Hannah, her pretty brown eyes taking in the photo of Marshall Fredricks that appeared at the top of the column. "I don't remember seeing him here."

"That's because I was the one who waited on him, remember?" Dylan grabbed his apron from a nearby wall hook and slowly tied it on, his disappointment at himself evident in his slumped shoulders. "If he'd been at your table, things would've gone a whole lot better."

"Or I would have gotten nervous and dumped his food on him," Raquel said kindly.

"Learn and move on," Hannah said. "That's all any of us can do."

"I will. I promise."

"Marshall's kind of cute, don't you think?" Raquel murmured. "You know, in a nerdy kind of way." She pointed at the clock on the far wall. "We open in ten."

And suddenly, any residual disappointment Hannah had over the less-than-stellar review was gone, pushed aside by the same thrill she'd felt at this exact moment every Tuesday through Saturday for the past five weeks. Were there things she needed to change and improve? Of course, as was the case for any new business. But in that moment, the anticipation of another evening at the helm of her dream was energizing.

Leaving Jacob to his final kitchen prep, Hannah followed Raquel and Dylan into the dining area. There, they split off in different directions, readying menus, making sure each table was set with utensil rolls and condiments, and filling the register drawer with varying bills and change.

Normally, hostess Elaine Wilby would be there to help things go even smoother, but she had the day off for a family birthday party—planned well ahead of time, unlike the Hot Spot's impromptu closure the previous day. She'd called Hannah to ask if she should come in, but Hannah had insisted that she stick with her original plan. Hannah was happy to cover hostess duties for the evening.

"So are you going to end our suspense now, or make us wait until closing?"

Setting the final denomination of bills into the cash drawer, Hannah glanced up to find Raquel watching her while moving around the dining room, scooting in chairs. "Suspense about what?" Hannah asked.

"Your day yesterday. You said it was something to write home about, remember?"

"Right. That." Hannah closed the drawer. "It's funny how quickly something in the forefront of your thoughts can get shoved to the back, isn't it?"

"All on account of that rotten food critic," Dylan grumbled.

"The paper says his name is *Marshall Fredericks*," Raquel reminded him, not unkindly.

Hannah couldn't help but smile at Raquel's dreamy expression. "Anyway, back to your question. You already know I spent the day helping at Miriam Spencer's house."

Dylan grabbed an order pad from behind the counter and slipped it into his apron pocket along with a pen. "Did you know there's a chance that the fire at her house might not have been accidental?"

Hannah gaped at the young waiter. "What are you talking about?"

"Chief Berthold was interviewed on one of the news channels today," Dylan said. "My mom had it on while I ate lunch. He said they're not ready to make a ruling on the cause of the fire just yet. If it was accidental, he would have said that, right?"

"Oh. Wow. I wonder what's going on with the investigation."

Raquel tucked an order pad into her own apron then tapped the time display on the register. "If you don't tell us what you found in the next two minutes, I'm going to be wondering about it all night."

Forcing her thoughts away from Dylan's unsettling words, Hannah nodded. "Right. Sorry. I found something in a secret compartment underneath a floorboard in Miriam's living room—something even *she* didn't know was there, yet someone else must have."

"Do tell!" Raquel checked her watch. "But quickly. We're under a minute now."

Hannah started to speak but stopped as a flash of movement on the other side of the large front window caught her attention. Two familiar faces with wide, goofy grins pressed against the glass.

Laughing, she waved, motioned for Dylan to illuminate the Open sign, and then pulled the handle on the front door. "Hey, Dad, Uncle Gordon. Are you here for dinner?"

"We are." Her father, Gabriel Prentiss, stepped inside the restaurant ahead of his brother, shook his gray hair from his brown eyes, and planted a kiss on Hannah's forehead. "My only daughter has finally made her way back home after too many years in California, so I'm going to frequent her restaurant as much as possible. You know this."

She returned Uncle Gordon's side hug as she spotted another man behind the pair.

"And we brought a friend. This is Bruce Davidson," Dad added.

Hannah held her hand out to a man she guessed to be a solid five or six years older than her father, who was in his midsixties, and softened her shake at the physical discomfort her grip clearly caused. "Welcome to the Hot Spot, Mr. Davidson. I'm Hannah, Gabriel's daughter."

"Call me Bruce." He nudged Dad. "I'd know you were this one's daughter even if he hadn't talked about you all the way here."

"Which he did," Uncle Gordon quipped. "And did. And did. And *did*."

Dad's smile defied his shrug of indifference. "Watch yourself, dear brother. I do keep a roof over your head, you know."

The group laughed, Bruce adding a shake of his shiny bald head.

"Are these two always like this, Hannah?" he asked.

"Always. How do you three know one another?"

Her dad smiled and said, "Gordon and I crossed paths with Bruce many times during our careers in the trades."

"Were you an electrician like my dad, or a plumber like my uncle?" Hannah asked.

"Neither." Bruce shook his head. "I was a carpenter. I worked throughout the entire county and a few of the neighboring ones, as well."

"Do you live here in town?"

"He spent his childhood here," Dad interjected, placing a hand on Bruce's shoulder. "And, like you, he's found his way back to Blackberry Valley."

Hannah grabbed three menus from the counter and held them to her chest. "Well, welcome home, Bruce."

"You as well, Hannah."

She motioned Raquel over and handed her the menus. "I'll turn you over to my favorite waitress, Raquel, but I'll be by to check on you in a little while."

Dad watched as his friend and his brother fell into step behind Raquel, and then he beamed at Hannah. "I don't think I'm ever going to grow tired of seeing you here, living your dream."

"Thanks, Dad."

"And as for that review in today's paper, you'll make that young man eat his words in no time."

She felt her smile falter and forced it back into place. "Thanks for the pep talk. Now go have fun with your friends."

"Any recommendations for your old man this evening?"

"Stay away from the Flame Squad on the appetizer menu. Your digestive system will thank me." She returned her father's wave and then turned to the door to greet the customer whose arrival had prompted Dylan to grab a single menu. "Welcome to the Hot…"

The rest of her greeting trailed away as her gaze moved between the familiar—and attractive—face of the Blackberry Valley fire chief and the large cardboard box he held in his strong arms.

Chapter Three

"Chief Berthold, hello."

"Liam. Please." He hefted the box. "I brought some things to help you combat the 'generic' comment."

She resisted the urge to groan. Instead, she took the menu from Dylan and gestured for the young waiter to greet the family of four who'd just entered. "You saw the review," she said to Liam.

"I did."

She raked her hand through her hair and tried to keep her tone light. "That stuff happens in my business. We'll get past it. Make adjustments. Address the issues."

"I love the Five Alarm Burger," Liam said staunchly. "With or without the fancy drawing on the plate. And I can always taste the jelly on it."

Hannah laughed. "Thank you. I'll let my chef know."

"And, as I said, perhaps I can help with that 'generic' comment." Liam indicated the box once again. "Do you have time to sit with me for a little bit?"

"I don't think so. We just opened, and there's always a rush first thing."

Raquel stepped behind the counter, quickly counted out five menus, and winked as she headed toward the door. "Dylan and I have this, Hannah. Go see what Liam has to offer."

Hannah faced Liam again, willing herself to focus on his face rather than the way his black hair shimmered in the early evening sunlight that streamed through the window. "I guess I can sit. For a few minutes, anyway."

She led the fire chief across the dining room to the corner opposite her father's table. There, they could have some quiet and she would still have a good vantage point to gauge the crowd and how long she could actually remain seated. When Liam was settled on the opposite side of the table, she set his menu down and waited as he reached inside the box that he'd set on the floor.

"I'm not sure whether you're aware of this, but before I was Blackberry Valley fire chief, and before my dad was, my grandfather held the position." Liam pulled out a folder and handed it across the table to Hannah. "And although we all like to hang on to things to varying degrees, my grandfather takes that to an extreme. He sees himself as the Blackberry Valley Fire Department's unofficial historian—so much so that he has to rent a storage unit to hold it all."

"And you?" she asked, amused. "How do you see him?"

"As the official Berthold Family Pack Rat."

Hannah's laugh brought a smile to Liam's handsome face, along with the faintest hint of a dimple. "Ouch."

"It's a family joke at this point. I tell him that same thing all the time. With the utmost respect and love, of course." Liam tapped the folder in her hands. "Take a look."

She set the folder on the table and flipped it open. Inside was a black-and-white photograph of a young, uniformed firefighter standing in front of the building that now housed her restaurant. His face, jacket, and hat were covered in soot. "Is this your grandfather?"

"It is. He'd just started with the department."

Hannah took in the wisps of dark hair peeking out from around the edges of the man's helmet and the eyes so like the ones watching her from the other side of the table. "You look a lot like him."

"The Berthold genes run deep."

"I can see that."

He tapped the badge depicted on his grandfather's uniform. "When I became chief last year, my mom gave me a shadow box that holds all three of our badges—my grandfather's, my dad's, and mine. It's really cool to see the subtle changes in the design from generation to generation. It hangs on the wall of my apartment."

"So it's a nod to your family's history as well as the Blackberry Valley Fire Department's," Hannah said.

"Exactly." Liam swept his hand toward the box. "Gramps put one of his patches in here for you, and so did I. And I've asked my dad to send an extra one of his, as well."

"I'm sorry to say I don't really remember your grandparents, but I do remember your parents. You know, seeing your mom at the grocery store, your dad in the town parade, that sort of stuff. And I know they were both there, at the church, when I came back for my mom's funeral." She heard the tremble in her voice and quickly moved the conversation into safer territory. "I take it your parents no longer live here?"

"They retired to Florida last year when I became chief."

"I see." Slowly, she returned her attention to the folder and the picture of Liam's grandfather. "When was this taken?"

"My guess is around 1962. Gramps was about twenty-two when he took his oath of office. But that picture was taken before he married my grandmother, so I can't be sure without asking him." A smile lifted the corners of Liam's mouth. "Once they got married, my grandmother recorded the year on every picture they took. Gramps says it was the librarian in her."

She turned the picture over, confirmed there was no date written on the back, and lifted her gaze to Liam. "Was your grandmother a librarian here in Blackberry Valley?"

"My grandmother was one of Blackberry Valley's early librarians," he said with unmistakable pride. "If you spent any time at the town library as a kid, you'd have known her as Miss Bridget."

Hannah's eyes widened. "Miss Bridget was your grandmother?"

"She was. She started at the library before she and Gramps married. Everyone already knew her as Miss Bridget, so she continued to have everyone call her that throughout her career."

"Wow. I loved her story time when I was little. She made every single story she read come to life."

Hannah set aside the picture of Liam's grandfather in favor of the next one in the stack—a large still of a two-story home on fire. She gave a low whistle as her gaze moved from the angry flames to the pair of firefighters in the foreground with a large hose. She was startled to recognize Liam's grandfather carrying a young child down a ladder from a second-story window. "Liam, this is an *unbelievable* shot!"

"Gramps and the other firefighters saved an entire family and their dog that night. One of many families he saved during his career." Liam gestured to the folder and the box. "This may all prove to be way more than you actually need, but it should help."

"More than I need?"

"You know," he said. "To counteract the 'generic' comment."

She stared from Liam to the open folder and back again. "Wait. Are you saying your grandfather is *lending* these to me to hang up in here?"

Liam smiled. "If you want to, he is."

"Want to?" she echoed. "I'm honored that you would entrust these to me. Liam, these are incredible. Thank you—you and your grandfather."

"It's our pleasure."

Curious, she looked at the back of the photograph depicting the heroic rescue. Sure enough, *1972* was written in pen along the bottom edge. "Your grandparents were married when this was taken, yes?" she asked, showing it to him.

"They were. About seven years by then. Which means my dad would've been five."

"I wonder if he went to school with the little boy your grandfather rescued," she mused.

"It's possible."

She returned the picture to the stack and closed the folder. "And you brought me all of this because of the review in today's paper?"

"Yes."

"Not my favorite moment of the week, I'm afraid," she admitted, her cheeks warming.

"I can't imagine it would be. But, like I said, I happen to like the Five Alarm Burger. A lot." He scanned the dining room. "And Dylan's a good kid. He'll figure it out. Rome wasn't built in a day."

"Thank you, Liam. I appreciate that. But why would you help me?" she asked.

"Because I can." He lifted the box onto the table and scooted it in her direction. "I took Gramps out to his storage place, and we spent about an hour going through it. If it's in the box, it's fair game. Use what you want and set aside what you don't. Oh, and in addition to the memorabilia my grandfather put in there, I collect antique firefighting equipment. Some of what I have might make for a nice display in here. Maybe on a rotating basis."

"You have enough for a rotating display, but your *grandfather* is the family pack rat?" Hannah teased.

He laughed. "Exactly. *He's* a pack rat. *I'm* a collector."

She rested a hand on the folder and the stack of pictures it held. "I'm really grateful, Liam. I'll take the utmost care of everything. Could you give me your grandfather's name and address so I can send him a proper thank-you note?"

"Sure," Liam said.

Hannah got Raquel's attention and borrowed her pen. She handed it to the fire chief along with one of the business cards from her pocket. After he wrote down his grandfather's name and address at a senior housing complex in nearby Cave City, she took the card from him and set it inside the box with the folder of photos. "Raquel, whatever Liam wants for dinner tonight is on the house."

"You don't have to do that," he protested.

"After *this*?" she said, wrapping her arms around the box of memorabilia. "It's the least I can do. You have no idea how excited I am to Blackberry Valley-up this place. It's going to be amazing. When I get everything displayed, will you bring your grandfather in to see it?"

Liam's dimple was back. "I will. He'll really enjoy that."

"Excellent." Hannah stood as Raquel took Liam's order. When she was gone again, Hannah lowered her voice. "Can I ask a question before I leave you to your meal?"

"Sure."

"I didn't see the afternoon news, and I haven't read the latest *Chronicle*. But Dylan said you don't know yet what caused the fire at Miriam's house. Is that true?"

"Oh, we know what caused it," Liam said. "We're just not ready to make a ruling on it."

She assessed his expression but couldn't get a read on it. "As in whether it was accidental or intentional?"

"That's right."

"But how could it be intentional?" she asked. "Miriam is a longtime local who's adored by everyone in this town."

"I know."

"Then why—"

But before she could finish her question, a voice interrupted. "Hannah?"

She looked over her shoulder to find Dylan holding a menu with a question in his gaze. "Yes, Dylan?"

"I have a customer at table six asking about an ingredient in the Fire Pump Pasta that I'm not exactly sure how to answer."

"No worries, Dylan. I'll take it from here if you'll put this on my desk for me." She traded the box for the menu and turned back to find Liam reading something on his phone. "Duty calls, I'm afraid."

He rose from the table. "For you and me, both, it seems."

"But what about your dinner?" she asked, walking him to the door.

"Have Raquel set it aside as a to-go order, if you don't mind. I'll either come get it when I'm done, or I'll send one of my guys over to pick it up." As they reached the front door, Liam met her gaze squarely, his brown eyes serious. "I assure you, if the fire at Miriam Spencer's house was intentionally set, Sheriff Steele and I will get to the bottom of the who and the why. You can count on that, Hannah."

Chapter Four

It was shortly after eleven o'clock that night when Hannah unlocked the door to her apartment above the restaurant and shouldered her way inside with Liam's box under her arm. She was tired, yes, but she was also happy—happy for the busy tables that had kept her and her staff bustling from open to close, and even happier for the smiles she'd seen on her customers' faces.

Tossing her keys onto the catchall table she'd found at a local vintage shop, Hannah made a beeline for her tiny living room and the ottoman her feet had been hankering for since the last counter had been wiped, the last trash can had been emptied, and the last tabletop bottle of ketchup had been filled in preparation for the next day. Part of her wanted to double back in the direction of the kitchen for a glass of water and maybe a snack, but the larger part of her wanted to get right into exploring the contents of Liam's box from the comfort of her couch.

She set the box on the center cushion and claimed the spot next to it for herself. Lifting her feet onto the ottoman, she allowed herself a contented sigh and then dug her hand into the cardboard box.

Beneath the folder of pictures she already knew about, she found a Blackberry Valley Fire Department helmet. Under that was a framed certificate commemorating the department's heroic actions in 1972.

There was a sleeve patch from Liam's grandfather with a center circle showcasing a helmet, a hose, and a bugle. *Blackberry Valley* was embroidered in white across the top, with *Firefighter* across the bottom.

Next, she pulled out the department's current patch from Liam, the inner circle now showing a ladder and axe where the hose had been six decades earlier. She set it on her lap and gently traced her finger across the newer details, envisioning the patch on the current fire chief's upper arm.

If she tried hard enough, she could sort of remember the Liam of her childhood. He'd been two grade levels above her, their ages, interests, and circles of friends making it so they had few reasons to ever cross paths.

Until Marshall Fredericks wrote his review.

She sagged at the memory of the food critic's harsh words. Did he have some valid points? Sure. But still, she'd wanted—*needed*—the first official review of her restaurant to be positive. She knew from her years of experience in the industry that the likelihood of getting a second chance with a food critic like Marshall Fredericks wasn't good.

Sighing, she reached into the box again, her fingertips touching another framed certificate, another sleeve of pictures, another—

Feeling the contours of a book with some sort of leathery cover, Hannah tugged out what looked to be a journal of some sort. She flipped it open, spotting Miss Bridget's name on the inside cover and then the most beautiful handwriting she'd ever seen.

August 6, 1962

As a young girl, my favorite place to go was the library. I loved the smell and feel of the books and the people and places those books introduced me to as I grew. While my friends would gaze out their windows and dream of what life would be like somewhere else, I lived it in the pages of the books I read. For me, there was no better way to spend my time than reading, and no better place to spend it than in a library.

That's why today was such a special day for me, a day I'll remember forever as the day one of my fondest dreams came true.

I am now a librarian in my new hometown, Blackberry Valley. Can you hear my smile in my words?

"Loud and clear, Miss Bridget." Hannah ran her finger down each line of the journal entry, recalling how happy she'd appeared even decades later reading stories to Hannah and other children. "Loud and clear."

How well she understood the joy of finally realizing a dream. She'd felt the same way the moment her very first customer walked through the doors of the Hot Spot five weeks earlier. It didn't matter that it had been her father. In fact, that made it all the more special. Because her father, more than anyone else except perhaps Lacy, knew how much that moment meant to her, how hard she'd worked to get to that place, how badly she wanted it to work.

She flipped the page, her curiosity aroused.

August 24, 1962

I'd planned to write every day, but work and life have kept me too busy, and I'm not sure that will change. Today, though, I can't help but write, as I'm afraid I'll burst if I don't.

While eating lunch on the library steps this afternoon, I felt, in one glorious instant, what Levin in Leo Tolstoy's Anna Karenina *felt when he first saw Anna.*

"He stepped down, trying not to look long at her, as if she were the sun, yet he saw her, like the sun, even without looking."

Because that's how I feel right now, nine hours after I saw the man I am certain I will marry.

He's tall, like my father, and his hair is just shy of black. He moved with purpose yet said hello to every person he passed. And when he felt me staring, he turned and met my gaze from the other side of the street, the sun sparkling off eyes I imagine were blue like the ocean, green like an emerald, or brown like the finest chocolate truffle.

I wanted him to cross the street, to speak so I could revisit the sound of his voice while writing this, but someone called to him, and I had to go back inside the library.

"We are asleep until we fall in love," *Denisov said to Sonya in* War and Peace.

If that is true, Denisov, I am awake now. And it's because of a boy named Patrick.

"Liam's grandfather," Hannah whispered. "And what was clearly the start of a decades-long love story."

Again, she ran her fingertips down the entry, delighting in the feel of the page. On some level, she knew she should stop reading. Liam's grandmother's journal had no doubt been added to the box by mistake. But despite the fatigue in her back and shoulders, legs and feet, she found herself continuing her perusal.

> September 14, 1962
> His eyes are brown. Like the most expensive chocolate.
> I know this, because Patrick too felt what I felt that beautiful day last month. Only instead of wondering and imagining as I thought I was destined to do, Patrick sought me out the first chance he had.
> There I was on the floor, reading Virgina Lee Burton's The Little House to Mrs. Harper's kindergarten class, when I looked up and saw him, standing by the front desk, staring at me as if I were a dream come true.
> I should've written about it that day, but my every day after work since then has been spent talking to him, sharing with him, learning everything I can about him and his brave choice to be a firefighter. And when I talk of my books and my patrons to him, he listens, truly listens, as if nothing on earth could be more important.
> He is everything I ever dreamed about.
> But that presents a problem.
> Because if I listen to my heart, I suspect I may very well break another's. Unfortunately, as sweet as Michael Spencer is when he tries so hard to get my attention, I know Patrick Berthold is the man I will marry.

Hannah sat up straight. "*Spencer?* As in *Miriam* Spencer?"

She shifted her focus, once again, to the top of the entry and the date—a date, by Hannah's calculations, that would've had Miriam being about twenty-one or twenty-two. Had Michael been Miriam's brother or—

"No." She shook the incorrect kinship from her thoughts. "Spencer is Miriam's *married* name."

She let her thoughts wander to the possibility of a cousin or an uncle or a brother of the man Miriam married before finally turning the page to the next entry.

February 5, 1963

It's been ages since I've written. I'll try to do better, but no guarantees.

All my life, when I've imagined a person in danger, I've pictured them being helped by some of God's angels on earth. Doctors, nurses, policemen, and firefighters like Patrick. Those are the professions I've always seen as synonymous with helping.

Today, though, for just a little while, I think I was able to add librarian to that list.

It was just after three o'clock when I heard the sniffles and the hitched breaths of someone crying. Besides the pair of teenage girls swooning over a picture of Warren Beatty in a magazine rather than working on their school project, I knew the one other person in the library was Libby's seven-year-old son.

Sure enough, I found him in the corner of the children's section.

I didn't know Libby was sick—really, really sick, if little Jerry is correct. And when he told me, it took everything I had not to cry too. But in that moment, helping Jerry was all that mattered. I sat on the floor next to him, gave him a tissue from my pocket for his tears, and held him until he stopped crying.

Patrick said that's often what it's like for him, as a firefighter. Putting his own fear aside to help someone else. I don't think what I did is even close to the same thing that Patrick does, but if I helped Jerry for even a little while, I'm glad.

Oh, and just so you know, I'm still head over heels for Patrick Berthold.

Hannah gave in to the yawn the hour dictated but remained seated, intrigue over the mysterious Libby and Jerry winning out over sleep.

June 5, 1963

I saw Jerry today. His mother's birthday was yesterday. He wanted to tell me about the cake he helped make for her, a cake she ended up being unable to eat because of how sick she is.

My heart aches for Libby, for her husband, and most especially for little Jerry. He wants her to walk him home from school the way she did before she got sick. He wants her to "laugh from her belly" at his jokes again. He wants to see her get dressed up in her prettiest dress for a special dinner with his dad like she used to. And he wants her to hug him really tight again.

I don't know what to say to him when he says those things. So I pray with him instead. Patrick says God will watch over Jerry and his parents, and I know he's right.

Hannah flipped to the next entry even as her eyes began to droop.

July 14, 1963

I can smell the fire. I can see the orange glow of the flames in the distance, and I'm afraid. Patrick has been to other fires since we started dating, of course, but this is a bad one. It's down on Courtland Street. I want to go, to see that Patrick is safe, but Dad says I have to wait. And pray.

Hannah turned the page, slumping back against the couch with relief as her gaze fell on the hastily scrawled addition she found on the next page.

P.S. Patrick is tired, but he's okay! He stopped by the house after the fire because he knew I would worry. He said he looked at my picture in his wallet as the fire truck arrived at the scene, that seeing me gave him extra strength.

Miss Bridget's words sent Hannah's thoughts off on a quick, mental tour of the pictures that gave her strength. The one of her at just three years old and her mom at the zoo, the smiles on both of their faces conveying the sheer joy they'd felt in that moment. The one of her and her parents at her college graduation. The one her father took of her and her mom, cuddled up together on a picnic blanket, reading.

"Seeing you gives me strength too, Mom," she whispered as her gaze traveled to the opposite page and another entry from Miss Bridget.

> *September 6, 1963*
>
> *I will never forget this day for as long as I live, and it's because of Patrick Berthold, the man I'm more certain than ever I will marry one day.*
>
> *When I left work this evening, Patrick was waiting at the bottom of the library steps with a bouquet of flowers—roses he'd spent some of his paycheck to buy! For me!*
>
> *He reminded me that it was one year to the day that he came in to find me at the library, and that it's a day to celebrate.*
>
> *Then he handed me a gift-wrapped box. My hands shook so badly that it took me a while to open it, but inside was the most beautiful thing I'd ever seen.*

Unable to stand the suspense, Hannah flipped to the next page and read the rest of the entry.

> *It was a ruby brooch! One that Patrick's grandfather gave Patrick's grandmother when they were courting. It's exquisite, like something a movie star might wear.*

"A *ruby* brooch?" Hannah said, bumping the back of her head against the couch.

> *He asked me to think of him when I wear it. I told him that would be easy, because even without the brooch, I already do.*
> *And that's true.*
> *I will wear it forever and always.*

Hannah thought back to the brooch she'd found at Miriam's the day before and wondered what the elderly woman and her son had chosen to do with it as she yawned, once again. It was time for bed. Every muscle in her legs and feet, arms and shoulders, told her that.

"Just one more entry," she said, stifling a third yawn with her hand.

Again, she turned the page.

> *November 15, 1963*
> *I don't know how Patrick will ever be able to forgive me.*
> *I wish I could explain it so he could understand, but how can I explain what I don't understand myself?*
> *I'm heartbroken.*

Dropping her feet to the ground, Hannah closed the book, angry at herself for continuing to read something that clearly hadn't been meant for her eyes. The journal was in the box Liam had given her, true, but she'd known the moment she started reading that the journal had nothing to do with the Blackberry Valley Fire Department.

Yet still she'd read, poking her nose into another family's private business.

Aggravated with herself, Hannah stood, carried the book into the entryway, and swapped it for her phone and the card she fished out of her back pocket. First thing in the morning, she'd get in her car and drive the journal out to Liam's grandfather at—

Her gaze traveled down the handwritten address she'd requested to a cell phone number at the bottom she hadn't. Beside the number was Liam's name.

Grabbing her phone, she plugged in his number and began to type.

Hi Liam. This is Hannah Prentiss. I found something in the box you gave me tonight that shouldn't have been in there. Can I bring it by the station tomorrow? If so, what would be a good time?

Chapter Five

Hannah stepped through the open garage door of the newer, more modern Blackberry Valley Fire Station on Thursday morning. In front of her, gleaming in the early June sun, was the town's largest fire truck, facing the road for a quick exit. To her right, on the wall beyond a smaller yet no less official vehicle, was a row of hooks on which the firefighters' jackets hung. To her left, laughter and the unmistakable aroma of frying bacon drifted through an open door that led to a long hallway.

Hiking her tote bag higher on her shoulder, Hannah called, "Hello? It's Hannah Prentiss. I'm—"

"You're looking for Liam, yes?"

She jumped and spun around to find a man about her age, with piercing blue eyes and a mop of dark blond hair, holding a cleaning cloth in one hand and a bottle of wax in the other. Beside him sat a dog with long black and tan fur.

"I didn't realize anyone was out here," Hannah said.

"I'm sorry. I didn't mean to startle you." The man tucked the bottle of wax under his arm and held out his hand for her to shake. "I'm Archer Lestrade, and this is Smoky, the firehouse dog. We work here with Liam."

Her breath finally steady once again, she reached down and offered Smoky her hand to sniff. When he wagged his tail, she scratched behind his ears. "Like I said, I'm Hannah Prentiss."

"Love your restaurant. It's exactly what this town needed."

"Thank you."

He pointed her toward the hallway. "Liam is in his office, which is the first door on the left. Though, if you're smart, you'll hit up the kitchen in back first and get yourself a piece of Colt's bacon. Kid's barely twenty-two and makes the best bacon I've ever eaten." He grinned. "Which might be worth keeping in mind should you decide to add a breakfast service at your place."

She held up her hands. "No. The Hot Spot is—and will remain—a dinner-only restaurant."

"You sure? Because seeing our rookie in an apron would be worth a few laughs for the rest of us at the station."

"But then you wouldn't be smelling it here, would you?" she pointed out.

"True." Archer chuckled. "Colt Walker is a good kid, a real asset to the department. But you can't let a rookie know that too soon or his head will swell."

"And you can't have that, can you?" she joked.

"Definitely not. I should get back to work and let you talk with Liam, but it was nice meeting you."

"It was. Thank you."

She followed Archer's directions to Liam's office. A peek inside revealed Liam standing over his desk, poring over a series of photographs spread across the metal surface.

"Liam?"

He looked up, concentration quickly giving way to a broad smile. "Hannah, hello. Good morning."

"Good morning."

He beckoned her into the office and the chair across from his desk. When she was seated, he followed suit, tenting his fingers in front of his chin. "So I'm guessing this is when you tell me you've found the remote control my grandfather mysteriously lost this past week in the box I gave you?"

She set her tote bag on her lap. "No."

"The spare key to his apartment he keeps saying he gave me but I know he didn't?"

She laughed. "No."

"Then I give up. What did you—"

A quick knock drew their attention to the door, where a young man stood with two plates of bacon. "Archer said you had a guest."

"I do." Liam stood and relieved the younger man of his burden. "Thanks, Colt."

"No problem, Chief."

And then the young man was gone, his footfalls quickly fading as Liam handed a plate to Hannah. "You want to try this. Trust me."

"I've heard." She set the plate on the closest empty desk space she could find then narrowed her eyes as her gaze landed on one of the pictures. "That's Miriam's house, isn't it?"

"It is," he confirmed.

Unable to resist, she stood and walked around to his side of the desk, her attention riveted on the rooms she and her friends had worked so hard to clean just two days earlier. Even to her untrained eye, it wasn't hard to pick out the room with far more than smoke damage. She tapped the middle photo with her finger. "The guest bedroom really took the brunt of the fire, didn't it?"

"Definitely."

"I thought the damage from the smoke throughout the rest of the house took a lot to clean. But *this*? It's amazing you were able to keep the flames from doing a whole lot more than smoke damage everywhere else. Even the damage that did happen out in the living room was minimal, comparatively speaking."

Liam nodded. "We had a few things working in our favor. First, we got there in under ten minutes, thanks to someone's keen sense of smell. Second, because of the age of the house, the doors are made of real wood, which makes them heavier than newer doors. Since the door to the guest room was closed, it helped hold the bulk of the fire in there, minimizing the spread. The old plaster walls also helped, in terms of vertical spread, which made it so this was more of a room-and-contents fire rather than the whole-house inferno it could've been."

In various photos, Hannah took in what was left of the bed, the nightstand beside it, and the dresser along the window's opposing wall. Several melted and charred objects littering the dresser's surface were identified on a neighboring sheet of paper—a picture frame, jewelry box, and makeup mirror.

"Wait. I get why you would have so many pictures of this room, but why are most of them focused on the area around the dresser?" she asked Liam.

"We're trying to figure out how the fire started."

She frowned at an earlier photograph showing the area on the other side of the bedroom, which had sustained far more damage. "Wouldn't you figure the fire started where there's the most damage?" she asked.

"Fires are interesting. They do all sorts of crazy things that can make an investigation tricky. When the ash is cleared away, that's when we find our clues. For example, a dark soot layer on a window often indicates a slow, smoldering fire, like what might happen from a cigarette that got dropped onto a couch—or, in the case of a bedroom—onto a bed."

"Miriam doesn't smoke," Hannah said.

"Of course not. I just used that as an example. A window with an abnormal cracking pattern would imply a hotter fire—something an accelerant would do."

"An accelerant?" Hannah echoed. "You mean like gasoline?"

"Yes." He took a bite of bacon. "But that isn't the case here either."

She sagged back in relief.

"A scene with more than one origin point is another indicator of a suspicious fire. How deep or thick the ash is can also give us clues. Thick ash can mean a hot, fast-burning fire."

"Which this wasn't, based on the minimal damage, right?"

"Correct." He used a strip of bacon to indicate a picture of the wall in Miriam's guest bedroom. "Fires burn upward, as you can see here along the wall behind what used to be a curtain. Fires that burn toward the floor get our attention because they likely mean a liquid accelerant was poured on the ground. The fire would follow it downward."

"Since you don't think an accelerant was used, does that mean you no longer think the fire was suspicious?"

"No, I'm not ready to say that yet."

Again, she took in the grouping of photographs showing the same dresser, her eyes drawn to what had clearly been a lamp at some point. "Are you considering the outlet this lamp was plugged into?"

"That's certainly something we examined early on. But if it had started in a particular wall outlet, the char pattern would've pointed to it as the point of origin."

"Interesting. So did you see that here?"

"No."

"Yet you have so many pictures of this dresser," she said, her curiosity piqued.

"We actually think the cause of the fire and the fire itself were on opposite sides of the room."

She looked from Liam to the photographs. "How can that be?"

"See if you can figure it out."

She studied the trio of pictures closest to his chair and noted the soot-covered object on which all three seemed focused. She took in the familiar oval shape, studied the mounded and blackened glass in the center, and then lifted her attention back to the handsome fire chief. "You think a *mirror* caused the fire?"

"It's a possibility."

"Which would mean it was more than likely accidental," she murmured. "Right?"

He polished off a strip of bacon and shook his head. "I'm not ready to take anything off the table yet."

"So you're being overly careful?"

"Probably. My grandfather grew up with Miriam Spencer. He'd want me to be sure."

His answer reminded her of the reason she'd come there in the first place. With one last look at the long, narrow dresser in Miriam's guest bedroom, she returned to her chair and the bacon she'd yet to eat. She took a bite, drew back, and stared at Liam. "Whoa. This is good. As in *really* good."

"Told you. I don't know what he does to it, but he can do it all day long as far as I'm concerned."

"I'm detecting a hint of brown sugar, and maybe even a little… maple. And I'm betting he made it in the oven." She took another bite as she took in the mixture of work and personal photographs hanging on Liam's office walls and displayed across shelves behind his chair.

She admired the moment he'd taken his oath of office, his face serious as two men who must be his father and grandfather watched proudly from their respective spots on the stage. Farther down on the same shelf was a picture of the Liam she remembered in elementary school—older than she had been at the time yet still a child. In the image, he sat behind the steering wheel of a fire truck, a too-big helmet on his head.

Below those, on another shelf, was a picture of Liam with his parents, and to its right, a black-and-white photograph of Liam's grandfather. Here, though, instead of rescuing a child from a burning home, Patrick Berthold had his arm around a vaguely familiar young woman with a big, bright smile and a brooch pinned to—

Hannah bolted upright in her chair. "Who is that?" she asked, pointing to the photo.

Liam took the silver-plated frame from the shelf. "You mean these two? These are my grandparents, from back when they were dating."

"Th-that brooch she's wearing!"

Again, Liam eyed the picture, his head bobbing ever so slightly as he did. "My grandfather gave that to my grandmother as a present on the first anniversary of their 'courtship,' as my grandfather always calls it. But then, a couple of months or so later, it disappeared, according to Gramps. Which is a shame because it actually belonged to my—"

"Great-great-grandmother," she said.

His eyes widened. "How did you know that?"

Hannah pulled his grandmother's journal from her bag. "From this," she said, setting it on his desk. "It's Miss Bridget's journal. I started reading it last night because you said everything in the box was fair game. But even so, I should've known it wasn't supposed to be in there after I read the first entry. Instead of being any sort of tie to the fire department, it was about her first day of work at the library. I kept reading anyway, and the second entry actually mentioned your grandfather, so I thought maybe it was supposed to be in the box, after all—that it was some sort of written account of his career. But then it didn't end up going that way, and I realized it had been put in the box by mistake. I'm sorry. I shouldn't have snooped."

He smiled at her. "Hey, no worries. You couldn't have known. I didn't know it was in there—or that it even existed."

"Can I see that picture?" she asked, pointing at the frame in his hand.

"Sure." He handed it to her.

Hannah stared at the brooch she'd read about the previous night, a brooch she knew with absolute certainty she'd held in her hands two days before.

"I—I know this brooch," she stammered. "I saw it the other day. In fact, I held it."

He stared at her. "What are you talking about? It's been missing for decades."

She pointed at the brooch in the photo. "I found it underneath a floorboard in Miriam Spencer's living room on Tuesday evening."

"Under a floorboard?" he repeated, as if he couldn't have heard her correctly.

"Yes. It was inside some kind of hiding place, a box with a lid. Only the lid wasn't on properly."

"I don't understand."

"Neither do I," she said.

"Did Miriam put it there?"

"I don't think so. Miriam seemed to be as surprised to see it as I was." She pressed her lips together, debating whether to continue. "But *someone* had to know it was there."

"What do you mean?"

"It was freshly polished," Hannah said. "The box was full of dust, but the brooch didn't have any dust on it."

He sprang up from his chair. "Are you saying there's *proof* that someone other than Miriam and her son was in that house recently?"

She looked from Liam to the brooch in the photo and finally back to the series of photographs spread across his desk—photographs taken to help him pinpoint the reason behind a fire in a house that bore evidence of a recent intruder.

Closing her eyes against a possibility she hadn't wanted to believe, she made herself nod.

Chapter Six

Hannah picked her way past the dozen or so hens that were inspecting the dirt and hay around her feet for any sign of a forgotten grain of food. She then squatted down in front of the cute red-and-white coop Lacy had built. A glance through the open chicken-size door revealed a handful of eggs and a hen standing guard over three more.

"The white one with the funky hair seems to be telling me she'll peck at my legs if I try to take her eggs," Hannah said, glancing over her shoulder at her best friend. "She won't, right?"

"If she does, she'll probably go for one of them, not both," Lacy replied with a grin.

Hannah scowled then returned to the chicken. "Your mama is so very funny, isn't she, Miss Chicken?"

"Her name isn't Miss Chicken. It's Martha."

"Of course it is."

"Seriously, though, she'll get out of the way when she sees your hand coming." Lacy moved the garden hose from one dish to the next, filling them with water for her birds. "Now, tell me again why you waited until you got out here to tell me the brooch you found belonged to Miss Bridget."

Gently, Hannah moved each of the unguarded eggs into the basket Lacy had thrust in her direction the moment she'd exited her car at her friend's farm. "You asked and I answered this same question less than five minutes ago."

"Yeah, but the part about not wanting to call on your way here doesn't compute. You call me from your car all the time."

Slowly, Hannah reached her hand toward Martha, flinched as the chicken reared back its head and seemed to be aiming its beak at her, and then sighed in relief as it abandoned its post beside the three eggs in favor of the coop's rear door and accompanying gangplank to the great outdoors. "You're right, Lacy, I do. But I think I needed to sit with the shock of it for a little while, you know? And I needed to process it before I could tell anyone about it with any kind of coherency."

"I suppose."

Hannah laughed. "If I could rewind to the moment I left, I'd have called," she said as she carefully added the last few eggs to her basket.

Lacy shut off the nozzle and stepped back to allow her two favorite hens, Hennifer and Eggatha, access to the water. "Now, before we get more into this brooch stuff, how were things at the Hot Spot last night?"

"It was good—really, really good," Hannah said. "Busy despite the *Chronicle*'s review yesterday. And then this morning, before I headed out, I tackled some necessary bookkeeping, ordering, and marketing work I needed to get done."

Lacy tugged the hose over to the bank of horse stalls inside the barn and began filling the first trough. "No moss grows under your feet. Not that it ever has."

Hannah carried the basket of eggs to the table and carefully transferred them to a waiting carton. Then she joined her friend at the second stall and trough.

"So, any guesses as to how Miss Bridget's long-lost ruby brooch ended up underneath Miriam Spencer's living room floor? Freshly polished, to boot?" Lacy asked.

Hannah hiked herself up onto a barrel and watched as Lacy dragged the hose to the third trough. "Haven't the foggiest. But Liam headed out to Miriam's the second I told him about finding the brooch there. He said something about calling Sheriff Steele on his way out. Beyond that, all I really know is the stuff swirling around in my own head."

Lacy released the nozzle sprayer and looked over at Hannah. "Which is?"

"Sixty-two years ago, Miss Bridget either lost the brooch Liam's grandfather gave her, or it was stolen." Crossing her swinging ankles, Hannah leaned against the shiplap wall at her back. "And since I don't know how she could've lost a brooch underneath a floorboard in a house she didn't live in, it makes more sense to me that it was stolen."

"Right. Who put it there? And how and why did they go back in and polish it?"

"And if it hasn't been there the whole time, when *was* it put there, and why?" Hannah added.

"You're thinking that someone would hold on to it all these years, only to hide it under a floorboard in someone else's house *now*?" Lacy asked. "That doesn't make a whole lot of sense."

"And feeling the need to polish something you stole sixty-plus years ago does?" Hannah pointed out.

"Right." Lacy coiled up the hose, placed it on a nearby hook, and then wandered over to the wooden upright across from Hannah.

"So let's look at what we do know. The house belongs to Miriam, and you said she was as surprised as you were when you pulled a ruby brooch from under the floor."

Hannah blew out a breath, the sound perking the ears of Razzle Dazzle, the horse in the second stall. "I did. And she was. But maybe it wasn't the brooch that surprised her. Maybe it was that I'd found it."

"What are you saying, Hannah?"

That was a good question. What was she saying? Miriam Spencer was an eighty-five-year-old woman. A member of their church and their women's group.

Holding up her hands, she tried to recant the accusation. "I didn't just say that, okay?"

Lacy frowned. "But you did."

"I know. And since I already have, do you happen to know what Mr. Spencer's first name was?" Hannah asked, straightening.

Lacy squatted to pet Mimi, the farm's pregnant goat. "As in Miriam's husband?"

"Or maybe the name or names of any brothers or uncles or male cousins he may have had."

Lacy scratched between the goat's horns, and Mimi pressed her head into her hand. "Why?"

"I came across something last night," Hannah said. "An entry in Miss Bridget's journal."

Lacy's fingers stilled, midscratch. Mimi gently nudged her hand. "Miss Bridget's journal?"

"I got it from Liam by mistake. It was in a box of Blackberry Valley Fire Department stuff he brought to display in the Hot

Spot. You know, to help me counteract one of the things Marshall Fredericks said in his review in the *Chronicle* yesterday."

Lacy smirked. "Oh? Do tell."

"Oh, stop." Hannah rolled her eyes. "Liam was just being a good guy who saw a way he could help a new business in town."

"I'm sure." Lacy squinted at Hannah. "Wait a minute. You said something about Liam heading out to his car to go to Miriam's after you told him about the brooch. Were you talking to him on the phone or something?"

"No. I didn't connect the brooch I found to the one Miss Bridget lost until I saw her wearing it in a picture behind Liam's desk."

"You were in Liam Berthold's *office*?"

"Yes."

"When?"

"This morning." Hannah held up her hand to stop the renewed smile on Lacy's face. "So I could give him back the journal I never should've had to begin with. That's all."

"I see." Lacy held up her index finger. "Quick side note. In answer to your earlier question, it was Michael."

"Excuse me?"

"Miriam's husband's name was Michael. It hit me out of nowhere just now."

"Are you certain?" Hannah asked.

"I am." Lacy slid her hand into the pocket of her overalls. "Care to share why the name of Miriam's late husband is important to you all of a sudden?"

Hannah pushed off the barrel and crouched to resume the scratching duty Lacy had abandoned, much to Mimi's delight. "I guess I'm wondering if *he's* the reason the brooch was under that floorboard."

"Why on earth would you wonder that?" Lacy asked.

Hannah kissed the top of Mimi's head and straightened. "He'd have had access to that room for starters, plus the time and access needed to craft the kind of compartment I found the brooch in. And according to one of the entries I read in Miss Bridget's journal, I think he had a crush on her in their younger years. But it sounds like Miss Bridget only had eyes for Liam's grandfather and vice versa."

Lacy's face scrunched with discomfort. "Did Miriam know he had a crush on another woman?"

"I can't answer that." Hannah crossed to Razzle Dazzle's stall and gazed at the chestnut-colored mare. "I didn't read enough of Miss Bridget's journal to know if she ever touched on that, and it seems like it would be a pretty insensitive thing to ask Miriam."

"But if Miriam's husband *is* the one who put the brooch there, wouldn't that mean he must have stolen it all those years ago?" Lacy asked.

"I think it would, yes. Unfortunately."

"But even if he did, how would that explain the freshly polished part? Michael Spencer passed away when we were both in college."

It was a valid point, and one that certainly required more thought. "I think I need to talk to Liam's grandfather. Maybe he can fill in some details to help me figure this out."

Lacy pulled a carrot from her pocket and offered it to Razzle Dazzle. "Do I need to remind you you're a restaurateur, not a detective?"

"No." Hannah watched the carrot disappear as Razzle Dazzle gave an appreciative whicker. "I'm just curious, I guess. I mean, I *am* the one who found the brooch under Miriam's floor. And I'm also the one who made the connection to Miss Bridget."

"True."

"Liam and his grandfather were nice enough to gather a lot of amazing things for the Hot Spot to borrow. Thanks to their effort, once I figure out how and where to display it all, people who come into the restaurant are going to get a glimpse of the real history of the Blackberry Valley Fire Department."

"Thus giving the old firehouse a more authentic feel." Lacy ran her hand down Razzle Dazzle's long neck. "A win for both your customers and you."

"Right. So if there's something I can do for the Berthold family in regards to *their* history, don't you think I should at least try?"

Lacy held up her hands in surrender. "Okay, you're right. I'll hold off on the detective jokes. Or I'll try to."

"Thank you."

"Just be careful, okay? And if you need a sidekick, let me know."

Hannah tilted her head. "A sidekick?"

"All the best detectives have them, don't they?" Lacy asked, hands on hips. "Sherlock Holmes had Dr. Watson, Hercule Poirot had Captain Hastings, Batman had Robin, and Nancy Drew had Bess and George."

"You don't think Neil would mind?"

"My husband would probably give you a medal."

"A medal, huh?" Hannah laughed. "What for?"

"Because if I'm out playing the role of sidekick in solving a real-life mystery with you, then I won't be calling him at work all the time asking him to bring me home another cozy mystery."

Hannah nodded sagely. "Ah, yes. The trials and tribulations of being a bookstore owner who married a bookworm." Lacy's husband, Neil, ran Legend & Key Bookstore, where he sold both new and used books of all kinds.

"What can I say?" Lacy asked. "I like to read."

Hannah checked the time. "I need to get going. Jacob asked me to meet him at the Hot Spot at one o'clock so he can try a new menu item out on me, and if I don't leave now, I won't have time to get out to Cave City and back in time to do that." She kissed Razzle Dazzle's nose and gave Mimi one last scratch.

Lacy walked Hannah to her car and gave her a hug. "What's in Cave City?"

"Liam's grandfather." Hannah opened the door of her Subaru Outback and slid in behind the steering wheel. "Patrick Berthold."

Chapter Seven

"Welcome to Clarkston Commons. How can I help you?"

Hannah stepped up to the welcome desk inside the sun-filled atrium and smiled at the petite redhead wearing a name tag that read RITA. "Hi. I was wondering if it would be possible to speak with one of your residents. I would've called him directly, but I only have his address, not his phone number."

"I can call his apartment. Who is the resident?" Rita asked, picking up her desk phone.

"Patrick Berthold."

Her full lips curving into a smile, Rita returned the phone to its base and gestured behind Hannah. "Mr. Berthold is right there. In the blue chair."

Hannah's gaze skittered across the trio of senior citizens chatting in the center of the sunlit room and came to rest on a startlingly familiar face in front of a floor-to-ceiling window. How she'd missed him upon entering the independent living facility's main building, she had no idea.

Because, studying him now, she couldn't help but feel as if she already knew Patrick Berthold. She knew his smile, the tilt of his head, the arch of his brow as he saw her looking in his direction. She was positive that, despite only having seen black-and-white photographs to date, the eyes now trained on her would be chocolate brown, as Miss Bridget had written.

Brown like Liam's eyes were.

Yes, she'd seen Liam's likeness in the photos of the Berthold family patriarch, but now she felt as if she were gazing into Liam's future as well.

Hannah smiled at the receptionist. "Thank you for your time, Rita."

"Of course."

Hannah threaded her way between the couch and a small café-style table to meet the man walking toward her, his steps slow but steady. "Mr. Berthold, hello. I'm—"

"Young lady, I'd know who you are even if my grandson hadn't told me you might be stopping by." Mr. Berthold captured Hannah's hand with his large warm ones and shook it. "You're Gabriel Prentiss's daughter."

She smiled, liking him already. "I am. But how did you know?"

"Your dad showed me a picture of you and Drew a few years ago when he fixed some wiring in the house I used to live in."

"Wait. My dad showed you a picture of his *kids* instead of Zeus?" she teased. "I'm amazed."

"Oh, I saw one of Zeus, as well. Cute dog." Mr. Berthold took a step back, gave her a quick once-over, and shook his head, grinning as he did. "And, even though you're all grown up now, I think there's a part of my brain that will always see you as a kindergartener."

"Why's that?"

"You played the role of a sheep in the elementary school's Christmas pageant that one year."

"Right. I fell asleep beside the manger. In the middle of the show," she said, grinning. "I've seen the video."

Mr. Berthold's answering laugh filled her heart with a warmth she felt clear down to her toes. "My wife and I were so tickled watching you that we might've missed our grandson carrying in the frankincense in his role as one of the three kings. But you won't tell him that, will you?"

"Your secret is safe with me," she assured him with a chuckle.

"Good." He again appraised her from head to toe, his smile fading as his gaze came back to hers. "You look so much like your mother."

Hannah felt the familiar catch in her throat. "Thank you. I've missed her every single day over the past eight years, but I feel as if she's always with me."

"As I feel about my beautiful Bridget." Mr. Berthold held his elbow out for Hannah to link with her arm and, when she did, he escorted her to a pair of chairs angled toward each other on the far side of the atrium. "It's a little quieter over here, so you can tell me what's brought you out to see an old man like me."

She started to protest his self-description.

He waved away his own words. "You're only old if you think you are, so we'll pretend I didn't say that. After all, I'm pretty sure I only live here to help the real old folks."

She laughed.

His answering smile made his eyes twinkle. "My wife would call you a breath of fresh air if she were here with us now. And she'd be right."

"Thank you."

"I hear you've opened a restaurant in my old firehouse and that the food is quite good. Clever name you've given the place too."

Her face warmed at the praise. "I have, and I'm thrilled to hear that."

"Did my grandson give you the box of things I put together for your walls?"

"He did," she confirmed. "And it's absolutely wonderful—thank you. It'll certainly elevate the theme, plus make it more personal for our town."

He sighed. "I just wish we could have taken care of it before that reviewer came in."

"At the end of the day, my restaurant is for my customers, not a one-time reviewer," Hannah said, as much for her own benefit as for his.

"That's a good attitude, young lady. Makes me want to come eat there even more."

"Give me a little time to get your wonderful memorabilia on display, and then I absolutely want you to come. And it'll be on the house when you do, as a small token of my gratitude."

Mr. Berthold snorted. "We'll see about that."

She grinned at him then caught sight of the clock. "Unfortunately, I can't stay long, as I have to get back to Blackberry Valley in time to sample a new dish my chef has concocted. So if it's okay, I'd like to ask you a couple of questions about something that was in the box Liam brought by for me yesterday."

"I'm listening."

"A journal of your wife's was in there by mistake, and I read some of it. At first, I thought it was in there because it would tell me something about your career, but—"

"It wasn't a mistake." Mr. Berthold set his elbows on the armrests of his chair and traced the outer edge of a flower on the upholstery with one finger. "I put it in there myself."

"Why?" Hannah asked, more puzzled than ever.

"Because a firefighter's career isn't lived in a vacuum, Hannah. It affects the spouse too." He stilled his finger and met her gaze. "I hoped you'd consider putting one of her entries in a frame to help customers understand that."

"I didn't realize...." She rested her head against her chair's cushioned back. "I felt as if I was snooping, so I returned it to Liam this morning. But yes, what you're saying makes sense now."

Mr. Berthold patted her hand. "I'll let him know I want you to have it. You mentioned you read some of it. How far did you get?"

"Three or four entries. But they were all from before you were married."

"Keep reading." Mr. Berthold lowered his hand to his lap. "Then you'll start to see why I put it in the box for you."

"Thank you."

"My pleasure, young lady." He leaned back in his chair. "Is there anything else I can help clear up for you?"

She took a deep breath to gather her courage. "When did your wife's brooch go missing?"

"My wife's brooch?" he echoed.

"Yes. It had a ruby and—"

He waved his hand. "Oh, that one. I gave it to her one year to the day from when we started dating. It belonged to my grandmother, and my mother gave me permission to give it to Bridget. Like me, my mother knew Bridget was the one I was meant to spend my life with. But why are you asking about it?"

She leaned forward, weighing the best way to answer. "I may have found it," she finally said, her voice as quiet as she could make it and still be heard.

His eyes widened. "You *what*? After all these years? Where?"

"In a compartment under a floorboard."

He sat up. "A floorboard *where*?"

"In Miriam Spencer's living room."

He stared at Hannah in a silence that quickly grew uncomfortable.

"I know that doesn't make sense, but—"

He scrubbed his hand across his face. "It makes more sense than you realize."

"Because of Michael?" she prodded. "Miriam's late husband?"

A flash of surprise crossed his face then faded. "That's right. You said you'd read some of Bridget's diary. Yes, because of Michael. But he and Miriam weren't married—or even dating." He gazed into the distance, seeming to age before her very eyes. "I wondered at the time if he had something to do with the brooch's disappearance, but Bridget was adamant that he didn't."

"Why did you suspect him back then?"

"Because everyone knew I'd given it to her and that she adored it. She wore it every day—to work, to the dance hall, on our walks, to church, you name it."

"And Michael liked her, right?"

A small smile softened his face. "How could he not? She was spectacular, inside and out."

Hannah smiled at the absolute conviction in the man's words and tone. It was beautiful to hear. "But why did you entertain the notion he'd taken her brooch? You and Miss Bridget had been dating for a year at that point. Surely he knew that, right?"

"He did. Everyone did. But the heart wants what it wants, and I knew from things he said that he was angry with me for winning her heart, and at her for choosing me."

"Instead of him," she mused.

"That's right. Perhaps he thought I'd get so upset over her losing a family heirloom that we'd go our separate ways."

She sat with his words for a moment, letting them combine with the image that had already begun to form in her thoughts. "Let me think out loud for a moment. If Michael Spencer *did* steal the brooch and hide it under the floorboards all those years ago, why wouldn't he eventually come clean and give it back to you or Miss Bridget once he met and married Miriam?"

"He already knew Miriam when Bridget's brooch went missing, but he didn't see Miriam that way yet." Mr. Berthold stared out the window, his thoughts clearly somewhere far beyond his physical view. "Now, as to your question about why he wouldn't give it back once he finally *did* notice Miriam, I can't answer that. Maybe Miriam would be the better person to ask."

"Miriam seemed as surprised by the brooch as I was when I found it," Hannah said. "I truly believe she didn't know anything about it."

His gaze returned to Hannah's. "Miriam might not have remembered it in that moment, but she definitely knew about it when I gave it to Bridget. *Everyone* knew about it. If they didn't happen to notice her wearing it, either her mother or mine filled them in."

Hannah smiled. "Small-town living at its finest, yes?"

"Indeed. But I must tell you, I take some comfort in knowing Miriam was unaware of my late wife's brooch being under her floor all these years."

"I can understand that." Hannah glanced down at her watch and grimaced. "I'm so sorry, but I really do need to start heading out if I'm going to make it in time to meet with my chef."

Mr. Berthold pushed himself to his feet. "I'll tell you one thing, Hannah. My Bridget would've *loved* the swirls."

"The swirls?" she repeated as she stood.

"The ones on the plate that the food critic didn't like."

Her laugh echoed around the large room as she took the arm he offered for their walk to the front door. "Did you hear that?"

"Hear what, my dear?"

"The 'I told you so' my chef surely just uttered in the wake of your words."

Mr. Berthold threw back his head and laughed then waved to a few of his fellow residents as they crossed the sunny atrium. "Then your chef knows what he's about. I'll tell Liam to return my wife's journal to you. If you see something in there that you'd like to use in your restaurant, feel free."

"Thank you."

"My pleasure." He stopped at the door. "Before you go, do you happen to know who has the brooch now?" His voice was wistful.

Hannah took his hand in hers and gave it a gentle squeeze. "I don't. But I'll see what I can find out, okay?"

"I'd be much obliged, Hannah." He pushed open the door for her. "You have truly been a breath of fresh air for me today. I hope our paths cross again soon."

She smiled up into the eyes that were so like his grandson's and stepped out onto the attractive walkway, which was lined with flowers in an assortment of reds, whites, and pinks. "Remember, you have an open invitation to the Hot Spot anytime. And if you come, I'll make sure Chef Jacob gives you some swirls in honor of Miss Bridget."

"I'd like that."

"I would too." Hannah started toward the parking lot—only to stop and turn around when a random thought struck her. "Do you happen to know who Michael Spencer hung around with back when you were courting Miss Bridget? A good friend? A cousin? Anything like that?"

Confusion furrowed his brow. "I can't say as I recall one way or the other. Once I hit sixteen, I spent as much time as I could at the firehouse doing whatever odd jobs they'd give me, both before and after school. I don't regret it, but it meant I didn't have a lot of time for clubs and other activities."

Hannah tried to hide her disappointment. "Right. Okay."

"Is there a reason you're asking?"

"Curiosity, I guess. And considering who I shared most of *my* secrets with at that age, in case someone else might have some answers for us." Hannah waved. "Thanks for your time. I'll be in touch. Soon."

Chapter Eight

There was something about the hour before opening that Hannah loved. Maybe it was the anticipation of what she hoped would be the Hot Spot's best night yet. Maybe it was the routine of prepping and the feeling of control it provided. Maybe it was the easy camaraderie of her staff that took the form of movie and book recommendations, silly jokes, and the sharing of their daily lives. But it was more likely that it was a combination of all of that.

Whatever it was, she recognized the joy she felt in her heart at this same time every day, and she was grateful.

"Care to share what—or *who*—is behind that smile?"

Hannah looked up from the silverware she was wrapping to find Raquel grinning at her across the table they were using for the chore. "This," she said, thrusting her hands toward the dining room at large, as well as at Raquel and Dylan. "All of it, including you guys. It just makes me happy."

"And here I was thinking it was about last night. Or rather, a certain guest we had last night."

Hannah plucked another napkin from the stack, set it down in front of her, and covered its center with one fork, one knife, and one spoon. "If you're referring to my dad, yes, I love having him come in for dinner with my uncle. And it was great that they brought a friend this time. But Dad *has* been here before. At least once a week since we opened, in fact."

Raquel and Dylan exchanged smiles across their own utensil-topped napkins. "That's not the who I was referring to, boss," Raquel said.

Hannah rolled the silverware inside the napkin, set it inside the waiting basket between them, and did her best to remember everyone who'd eaten at her restaurant the previous evening. "Who did you—wait! Are you talking about Liam?"

Raquel and Dylan again exchanged knowing smiles with Dylan victoriously lifting his latest silverware roll above his head. "Ha! Not 'Chief Berthold'?"

"He *told* me to call him Liam," Hannah protested.

"Did he? Fascinating."

Hannah made a face at her server. "Raquel, please. He came in for dinner like everyone else last night."

"Hmm." Raquel grabbed a fork, spoon, and knife and wrapped them in record time. "Dylan, did Hannah ask you to put gifts from anyone else in her office last night?"

"Nope."

Raquel raised her eyebrows at Hannah. "Inquiring minds are dying to know what that was all about."

Hannah rolled her eyes. "Liam brought me a box that I asked Dylan to put in my office. Then he and I sat and talked while he walked me through what was in the box. And just so we're clear, my nosy little staff, he also saw that review in yesterday's paper."

Raquel's smile drooped, as did Dylan's shoulders.

"For what it's worth, *he* didn't have any issues with Jacob's plate swirls," Hannah said.

"See?" interjected the chef from the kitchen.

"And he thinks you're getting better every time he's here, Dylan." Dylan's smile was back.

"But he thought Marshall's comments on the theme weren't wrong." She glanced around the dining room at the spots she'd already picked out for some of the new pictures and memorabilia. "That's why he brought me the box. He and his grandfather filled it with photos and patches and other things I can display in frames or shadow boxes. They'll be a nod to the Hot Spot's history as an actual firehouse."

Jacob's voice filtered out to the dining room again. "Take *that*, Marshall Fredericks!"

"I need to pick up some frames and get everything ready to be hung," Hannah finished, chuckling. "That's my plan for after church on Sunday or maybe Monday."

"Fine," Raquel said with a sigh. "We stand corrected. But you have to admit, the fire chief is rather handsome. And apparently considerate."

Unable to argue either point, Hannah took the full silverware basket from the table and carried it to its spot beside the menus at the welcome stand, her waitstaff trailing her. "Now, to change the subject, can I ask you two a question?"

"Of course. What's up?" Raquel asked.

"I'm curious about someone's friends in high school. Figuring out who they were, how close they were, stuff they may have done together—that sort of thing."

"Stalk their social media accounts," Dylan said. "You'll be able to figure out all of that in record time."

Hannah pulled out a half-full basket of crayons and handed it to him. "This is for someone who would've been in high school sixty-plus years ago."

"I'm out," Dylan said, lifting his hand in surrender. "Pretty much my entire existence has played out on social media."

Raquel rolled her eyes. "Kids these days."

"Oh, please." Dylan topped off the basket with crayon boxes for their youngest customers and then handed it back to Hannah. "And you're, what? Three years older than me?"

"Four, thank you very much."

The din of the kitchen paused long enough for Jacob to poke his head out and say, "High school yearbooks. Have you ever looked at your parents' yearbooks? It can be a rather eye-opening experience."

Hannah made a beeline for the open kitchen doors. "That would be a brilliant idea if I didn't think asking to see someone's yearbook would necessitate me giving more information than I'm ready to."

"I'm pretty sure my yearbook is in the Blackberry Valley Public Library." Jacob bent over the counter, ran his index finger down the menu of the evening's specials, and then stepped back, clearly pleased with himself. "Yours too, I imagine. And no one would ask questions about your going through those."

"The library," Hannah murmured. "I hadn't thought of that."

She hurried to her tiny office on the far side of the kitchen. She still had time to make a call. She grabbed her cell phone, searched for the number for the local library, and dialed.

"Good afternoon. Blackberry Valley Public Library, how may I help you?"

"Hello, Mrs. Cooke? This is Hannah Prentiss."

The head librarian's smile was practically audible through the phone. "Why, Hannah! Hello, dear. How are you?"

"Wonderful, thank you."

"Are you enjoying being back in Blackberry Valley?"

"More than I can say."

"Ted and I have been meaning to get to your restaurant for dinner, but it hasn't happened yet. We will though," said the librarian. "Now, what can I do for you?"

"Does the library have yearbooks from the various graduating classes of Blackberry Valley High School?"

"We do indeed."

There was no denying the surge of excitement that went through Hannah at her answer. "How far back do you have?"

"Since the first graduating class in 1945."

"That's exactly what I was hoping you'd say. And you have them all since that first one?"

"We do," Mrs. Cooke said. "They've become bigger and more elaborate over time, of course, but we have them all. Is there a specific one you'd like me to set aside for you?"

Hannah started to say yes but quickly realized she didn't know exactly which year or years she would need. "No, you don't need to set anything aside. I'll find what I need when I have a moment to stop by."

"Perfect," Mrs. Cooke said. "Is there anything else I can help you with?"

"No. You've already told me exactly what I wanted to know." Hannah's phone beeped, and she checked the screen to see Lacy's name on an incoming call. "Anyway, thank you, Mrs. Cooke. I hope you have a great rest of your day."

"You too. I'll see you soon, either at your workplace or mine."

Hannah ended the call and made her way through the kitchen to the dining room. As she answered the incoming call, she waved to Elaine, the restaurant's hostess, whose brown hair was swept back from her kind and welcoming face.

"Hey, Lacy, I only have a few minutes before we open. Is everything okay?"

"It is. But I wanted to ask you about a young woman who stopped out at the farm today asking for work," Lacy said over the bleating of Mimi the goat in the background. "It's not that I can't use the help—I always can—but I don't know anything about her and was wondering if maybe you do. Her name is Penelope McIntosh."

"Penelope McIntosh? I'm sorry, Lacy. I can't help you with that one. I don't know her."

"I know her," Dylan piped up from his spot beside Elaine. "Well, I've met her anyway. I talked to her at Jump Start Coffee before the Hot Spot opened. The guy behind the counter was telling her about the Help Wanted sign you had up, and I told them I got the job." There was no small amount of pride in his tone.

"The 'guy behind the counter' over at Jump Start Coffee is my brother, Zane," Jacob called out.

"Really? I didn't know that. That's cool, Chef." Dylan looked back at Hannah. "Anyway, I'm guessing it's the same person. Penelope isn't exactly a common name."

"Did you hear that, Lacy?" she asked into the phone. "Dylan thinks he met her, but he doesn't know her."

"Okay. I wasn't sure if maybe Miriam had said anything about her to you. I hate to call and bother her along with everything else she's already dealing with right now."

"You lost me, Lacy," Hannah said. "What does Miriam have to do with this Penelope person?"

"Because up until the fire, Penelope was employed by Miriam."

"To do what?" Hannah asked, surprised.

"She helped around the house with chores, errands, gardening, and other stuff like that. But now that Miriam's son is staying with her, Penelope's services aren't needed." Hannah heard another, more insistent bleat from Mimi. "She's offering to help me out around the farm, at least until Miriam needs her again—if that happens."

"I wish I could help."

"Hey, Hannah?"

Hannah glanced at Raquel, who nodded toward the window, where curious faces peered in. "I'm sorry, Lacy, it's four o'clock. I have to go."

"Of course. Have your most successful night yet," Lacy said.

"Thanks, friend."

Hannah ended the call then silenced her phone and slipped it into her pocket as she switched on the Open sign. Dylan unlocked the door to the first few customers of the night—faces she knew by sight if not by name.

Like the well-oiled machine they were becoming, the team fulfilled their roles. Elaine greeted the first party of four, gathered up the needed menus and utensil rolls, and then led them to a table in

Raquel's section. Then, while Raquel exchanged pleasantries and took their drink orders, Elaine returned to the welcome stand and Dylan's first customer of the night.

Minutes after their first customers arrived, Liam walked through the door.

"You're back," Hannah said, grabbing a menu for him. "Hopefully you can make it through your meal from start to finish this time."

Liam's dark eyes sparkled, the light bringing out flecks of gold in their depths. "As tempting as that sounds, I'm actually not here to eat this time."

"Oh?"

"I'm here under direct orders to see you."

Chapter Nine

"Direct orders?" she echoed. "Who from?"

"My grandfather."

At the mention of Patrick Berthold, she smiled. "I actually spent a little time with him earlier today."

"Trust me, I'm well aware. You made quite an impression on him." Liam held up his grandmother's journal. "He chastised me for accepting this from you. Said he'd disown me if I didn't give it back *today*."

"He said he'd disown you?" She chuckled. "That's kind of harsh."

"Not in so many words, but it was implied," he admitted, grinning. "As I said, you made quite an impression on him."

"I'm flattered."

She hooked her thumb over her shoulder in the direction of a booth in a corner of the dining room. "Do you have a minute to sit?"

"Sure."

"Perfect." She led him to the booth and waved Dylan over. "What can we get you to eat?"

Liam tapped his watch. "I only have about forty minutes."

"We can send you back to the station with it if you don't have time to eat it all here," she offered.

Liam smiled up at Dylan. "What do you recommend?"

"I'm partial to the Inferno wings myself," Dylan said.

Liam raised an eyebrow at Hannah. "*Inferno*?"

She grinned. "The hottest ones we have."

"And the least hot?" Liam asked the young waiter. "What are those called?"

"Glowing Embers are our mildest wings, Flamethrowers are our middle-of-the-road wings, and Inferno are the ones that'll make your eyes and nose run," Dylan said.

"I'll take the Flamethrowers, please." When Dylan stepped away, Liam set his grandmother's journal on the table and pushed it across to Hannah. "For you."

She pulled the book closer and gently ran her hand across its cover. "Thank you. I felt so bad when I thought I'd read things not intended for my eyes, but now that I know it wasn't a mistake, I can't wait to read more."

"Sheriff Steele met me out at Miriam's after what you told me in my office this morning," Liam said.

"Was he annoyed we hadn't told him about finding the brooch on Tuesday?"

"He wasn't thrilled, but he realizes there's no way you could've known it was stolen from my grandmother sixty-plus years ago."

A burst of sunlight flashed across their table as the front door opened and a group of six uniformed men walked in—two deputies, two EMTs, and two firefighters she recognized from the firehouse that morning. "The blond one is your friend, right?" she asked, nodding toward the group. "Archer?"

"Archer Lestrade. We've worked together for coming up on ten years now."

"And the other is the bacon-making genius Archer thinks I should hire if I ever decide to make the Hot Spot a breakfast place. Which, for the record, I won't."

Liam laughed, drawing the firefighters' attention as Elaine led the group toward Raquel's section. "That's Colt Walker, and he's a dynamo in and out of the kitchen. I wouldn't speak to you ever again if you stole him from us. Or Archer, if you did so on his recommendation."

"Good to know."

Archer split off from the group and came to their booth. "Hannah, good to see you again." He smirked in Liam's direction. "I'd ask if you want to join us at our table, Liam, but I know *I* wouldn't if I were you."

Hannah resisted the urge to press her hands to her rapidly warming cheeks and instead took a sip of water from the glass Dylan had set in front of her before disappearing toward the kitchen once again.

But then Archer's expression sobered. "You might want to check your email when you get a chance, Liam."

"Why's that?" Liam asked.

"The county fire marshal called with some news for you."

"Why didn't you tell him to call my cell?" Liam demanded.

"He was going into a meeting," Archer replied. "So he said he'd email you instead."

Liam scowled at him. "And why didn't *you* call me?"

"I told the marshal I'd give you a call as soon as we were off the phone, but he told me it wasn't all that urgent. He just wanted you to check it out sometime this evening so the two of you can discuss it tomorrow morning."

"What time is he calling?" Liam asked.

"He's not. He's coming into the station at nine." Archer stepped aside to give Dylan access to the table once again—this time to set Liam's wings on the table. "I'm guessing it's about the Spencer fire."

Drawing in a quiet breath, Hannah set her sights back on Liam in time to catch his quick nod.

"Anyway, I should probably leave you to your dinner so I can get to ordering my own." Archer pointed at Liam's wings. "Those look amazing. What are they called so I can get some too?"

"Inferno wings."

Hannah opened her mouth to correct Liam but stopped when he subtly shook his head at her.

"Perfect. Thanks." Archer smiled at Hannah. "It's nice to see you again, Hannah."

"You too, Archer." When he was gone, Hannah chuckled. "Inferno, huh?"

Liam grinned. "I like my bacon."

"I guess you do."

He gestured to the wings. "Help yourself. Please."

She held up her hands. "I can't. I'm on the clock."

"It's your own clock, though, right?"

"It is. But I'll eat later, after we close."

He stilled his hand on his first wing. "You're open until ten, aren't you?"

"We are. But that's okay. Please enjoy your food." She traced the edge of Miss Bridget's journal with one finger as he dug in. "If it turns out the fire at Miriam Spencer's was deliberately set, do you think it could be related to the brooch and its recent polishing?"

He wiped his hands with his napkin, took a long drink from his water glass, and then sat back, leveling his gaze on Hannah. "It certainly tells us someone was in that house who shouldn't have been. But if what Gramps told me on the phone a little while ago is right, then I don't know what to think. About any of it."

"Because Michael Spencer is dead?"

"For starters, yeah. I mean, if Miriam's late husband really did steal my grandmother's brooch all those years ago and he's been dead now for more than ten years, who else knew where it was, and why in the world would they break into Miriam's home to polish it?" Liam selected another wing. "It makes no sense. It stands to reason that the intruder who polished the brooch also set the fire, because how many intruders can one house have? But on the other hand, it doesn't make sense to me that anyone would break into a house to polish a hidden brooch, hide it again instead of taking it, and then set a fire. After all, if they cared enough to polish the brooch, why would they leave it hidden and then put the hiding spot in danger?"

It did, indeed, make no sense. Unless...

"There's still no guarantee the fire was set, right?" she asked.

"Right. Though the email from the county fire marshal might prove otherwise."

She sat with his words for a moment as he ate two more wings, chasing each down with a long pull from his water glass.

"These are great, but Archer is going to kill me if the Infernos are hotter than the Flamethrowers," he said. "And the water doesn't really help, does it?"

She chuckled. "Nope. And they are, much hotter. Trust me. Jacob can be overzealous."

"Well, that's what happens to traitors, I guess." Liam ate his last wing and then reached for the handwipe packet beside his plate. "Hey, my grandfather mentioned that you asked about Michael Spencer's friends he had when he was a boy. Any reason?"

She'd wanted to play that hand close to her vest, but after all, Liam was a member of the family who owned the brooch. If anyone deserved to be privy to anything she learned about it, he did. "I started thinking of people Michael might have told about the brooch if he did take it, and a close friend was the first thing that came to mind. I could ask Miriam who his friends were when he was in his late teens and early twenties, but I don't want to subject her to the possibility of Michael's involvement prematurely. She's had enough already with the fire and finding a brooch hidden under her living room floor."

"That's considerate of you," Liam said.

"Well, this whole situation is tricky," Hannah said. "Does Miriam know that the brooch I found belonged to your grandmother? And that it was stolen sixty-some years ago?"

Liam nodded. "Sheriff Steele and I informed her of that this morning when we went to see her."

Hannah slumped back against the booth. "How did she take it?"

"Like a champ. Handed it over immediately, no questions asked." Liam grabbed a piece of celery from his plate. "Tom, her son, was a bit more hesitant. He questioned whether it belonged to my family or his, since it was in his mother's house. But Miriam told him to quit being so contrary, and he did."

"I guess that's good. But now what?"

"What do you mean?"

"Is the sheriff going to investigate how the brooch got there?" Hannah pressed.

"They dusted for prints, but I don't think they'll put too much effort into anything beyond that. The department doesn't really have the time or the resources to spend on a sixty-year-old crime, especially when the brooch has been recovered." Liam finished off his celery stick and picked up the second one. "Getting back to what you were saying a moment or two ago, don't you think Miriam would know who her husband's friends were then, since they grew up in the same town?"

"I imagine she would. But I think I can find out the same information on my own without bothering her."

"How?"

"His high school yearbook," Hannah said. "Evangeline Cooke says the library has one from every graduating class."

Propping his elbows on the table, Liam leaned forward. "Interesting idea. Do you know when he graduated?"

"I know he was about the same age as your grandfather."

"So, 1958? Give or take a year?"

"That was my guess as well," she said.

"Smart. But I have a question."

She smiled. "Shoot."

"Why the interest in this?" he asked. "For you?"

It was a fair question, and one she took a moment to sit with before trying to formulate her answer in a way that would make sense to the fire chief. "Several reasons, I guess. I'm the one who found the brooch. I'm the one who realized it was your grandmother's. And the entries I read in your grandmother's journal made the brooch, and your grandfather giving it to her, all the more meaningful to me. I feel connected to its story somehow."

He studied her in silence, his thoughts as much a mystery to Hannah as the newly found brooch itself. At last he asked her, "Will you keep me informed about what you find?"

"I will. Will you do the same for me?"

He sat back. "About the fire, you mean?"

"Yes."

"I'll tell you as much as I can. Okay?"

She nodded. "I appreciate it."

A commotion erupted in the center of the dining room, and Hannah twisted around to see Archer lunge past his water for the glass of milk Raquel had brought out with his order. "Hot!" he wheezed between gulps while laughter erupted around him.

Glancing back at Liam, Hannah felt her lips twitch with amusement. "I hope you're proud of yourself, Chief Berthold."

Liam gave her a smug smile. "I repeat. I like my bacon."

Chapter Ten

The next morning, Hannah reached the front door of the Blackberry Valley Public Library in time to hear the lock disengage at exactly nine o'clock. The library was housed in a squat, unassuming building made of brick. The architecture didn't have as many flourishes as other libraries she'd seen, but it had plenty of windows to flood the interior with natural light.

She quickly made her way up the remaining steps to the very same door she'd walked through countless times in her childhood. When she reached it, she pulled on the handle, stepped inside, and paused. Lifting her chin, she inhaled the potpourri of smells that were as much a part of her surroundings as the shelves of books lined up like soldiers across the library's expansive main room. She smelled the books, the nostalgic mustiness she would forever equate with the old-school card catalog, the vinyl backing of the story-time carpet squares piled in a nearby corner, and the faint hint of coffee, no doubt coming from the mug on the information desk.

Why was she just now coming here after being back in Blackberry Valley for months? It was a valid question, for which her mind could provide no explanation beyond the busyness of buying and moving into the old fire station, renovating the building for the Hot Spot, and finally pressing start on the business of owning her own restaurant.

Then, as she stepped forward, she was hit with the real reason she'd waited. Memories of her mother were everywhere in this building

How many times had her mother helped her choose a carpet square for story time while whispering, "You're going to love this book, Hannah"?

To her right, where the card catalog still stood, she recalled her mother's helpful presence as she learned how to use it for school papers and assignments.

And, in front of her, under the checkout sign, her mind's eye inserted her warm, beautiful mother with a stack of books so clearly that Hannah had to blink a half dozen times before she was once again the only patron in the room.

"Hannah!" Mrs. Cooke hurried toward her, wearing a broad, familiar smile.

Hannah returned the smile. "Hello. It's so good to see you again."

The librarian pulled Hannah in for a quick hug and then released her for a head-to-toe inspection. "Oh, Hannah, you are truly the spitting image of your mama. How are you?"

"I'm well. Thank you. And you?"

"No complaints." She looped her arm through Hannah's and escorted her toward a series of chairs lining a nearby study table. When they were both seated, she continued. "I know I'm getting older with each passing day, but, for some reason, it still catches me by surprise when I realize others are, as well. Especially ones I remember since they were teenagers, like you."

She laughed. "I'm not a teenager anymore, Mrs. Cooke."

"Which means I want you to call me Evangeline. Please. 'Mrs. Cooke' was okay back then, but now that you're in your thirties, I don't really want to think about that age difference anymore."

Hannah nodded. "I hear what you're saying. But if I slip and call you Mrs. Cooke now and again instead of Evangeline, it's because old habits die hard."

Evangeline smiled. "Fair enough. Now, I imagine you're here to see those yearbooks you asked about on the phone yesterday?"

"If I can."

"Of course." The librarian pushed back her chair, stood, and motioned Hannah into a smaller room accessible through a door on their right. Then she spread her hands toward the assortment of shelves—some tall and narrow, others short and wide. "This is our local history collection. In addition to things like the yearbooks, we also have books by local authors about the Blackberry Valley of yesteryear, as well as reference material regarding town services, residents, and more."

Hannah scanned the well-stocked room before returning her full attention to Evangeline. "I don't remember this room being here when I was growing up. Did the town do some sort of expansion?"

"No. It's original to the building but was repurposed to be patron space during the library's renovation five years ago."

"What was it before that?" Hannah asked.

"A staff lunchroom. But, since my colleagues and I either eat our lunch at the information desk or outside on the steps if the weather is nice and no one is here, it felt like a waste of space. Now it serves as a special way to celebrate our little town." Evangeline crossed to a long, two-shelf unit beneath a window and ran her hand across a series of bound books of sequentially larger sizes and similar color scheme. "Here are the yearbooks. The oldest ones are on the left, the newest on the right. See?"

Hannah stepped closer. "Seems simple enough."

"Some people think I should lead with the most current year, but it makes more sense to me to do it this way, and I've never had patrons complain that they can't find what they need." Evangeline, again, spread her arms wide, this time toward the yearbooks rather than the room in which they were housed. "So what year are you interested in seeing? Your own? Your father's?"

Before Hannah could figure out how to reply, a child's happy squeal sounded from the main room.

"Oh! I think the little ones are starting to arrive for Friday morning story time. Are you okay to find what you need without me?" Evangeline asked.

"I think I am."

The librarian pointed to a small round table and a pair of chairs. "At this time of day on a Friday, you should have this room and that table to yourself, at least for a while. This particular story time is with toddlers, so the parents stay in the main room with me the whole time. I'll come and see if you need anything else afterward if I get a chance. Otherwise, make sure to stop and say goodbye before you go, okay?"

"Will do. Thank you, *Evangeline*." Hannah placed special emphasis on the name, making the older woman smile.

Evangeline crossed to the door. "I've run into your father a few times since you moved back, and he is positively overjoyed to have you in town. He's missed you."

"I've missed him too," said Hannah. "Very much." And it was true. She had missed him every day of her life in California. But she'd convinced herself that she couldn't give in to her homesickness until she'd learned what she could about every facet of the restaurant business so she could run her own.

Another metallic click echoed in the distance, followed by the sound of more sweet voices happily chattering away.

"I'll leave you to it then, Hannah." With a quick wave, Evangeline stepped out of the room, to the raucous delight of what sounded like several toddlers on the other side of the wall.

Hannah grabbed the yearbook labeled 1958 and carried it to the table. She settled into a chair and flipped back the cover to reveal a black-and-white photograph of the same high school building she had attended twenty years before.

The book was thinner than its more modern counterparts, but the contents were essentially the same. She scanned the captions paired with sophomore and junior group photos but found no specific names—just the event or club meeting or classroom in which they'd been taken.

Next came a few pages of casual shots of older students, but without context, no one stood out. She flipped forward until she reached the pages devoted to the graduating class of 1958, listed in alphabetical order. Two people down, she recognized a familiar face.

Were there wrinkles now where, sixty-seven years earlier, there had been none? Sure.

Was the excitement she saw in the youthful eyes in front of her now recorded in lines across the once-smooth forehead? Without a doubt.

But the steady gaze and the genuine smile that greeted her from the page of the yearbook were the same ones that had greeted her at Clarkston Commons the previous day. Beneath the then-senior's name and picture was a six-word pledge the Berthold patriarch had gone on to live by: *I promise to protect and serve.*

"And you did," she whispered as her mind's eye cycled through the many pictures taken during the man's career that would soon hang on the walls of the Hot Spot. "As did your son. As does your grandson."

She took one last look at Patrick Berthold's eighteen-year-old face and then turned the page, her gaze taking in pictures as she brushed her index finger across last names for the right letter.

Stilling her finger at the name *Michael Spencer*, she studied the accompanying photograph. Even with the black-and-white coloring of the picture, she could tell that Michael Spencer had been blond in his teens. His jaw was square, his lips full, his eyebrows bushy. And while he too smiled, just as the rest of his fellow graduates had done, his somehow seemed guarded and shy.

She paused a moment to see if the younger version of Miriam's husband would give off a sense of familiarity, but there was nothing. If she'd had any interactions with the man prior to his death, they'd left no memories.

She glanced at the space beneath his name for a quote.

"What?" she said aloud, glancing back at Michael Spencer's young face. "No words of wisdom? No prediction for your life? No inside joke?"

Then again, what difference did it make whether he'd included a quote or not? She now knew what Miriam's late husband had looked like just a few years before Miss Bridget's brooch had gone missing. Which meant she could search for him elsewhere in the yearbook, in the hopes of tying him to a particular friend or two who might know whether Michael had a secret.

Flipping through the rest of the graduating class, she stopped on a collage of stills and slowly scoured each one. Four girls laughed during a hula-hoop contest in the school gymnasium. Two boys faced each other across a chessboard, their expressions serious, their attention riveted on the game. Patrick Berthold hung on every word during a firefighter's classroom visit.

Two boys perched on a classroom windowsill, one's mouth opened wide with laughter while the other's head was tilted back, laughing up at the—

Leaning forward, she recognized the second boy as Michael Spencer. Then she inventoried every identifiable feature of the other boy. Short. Stocky. Freckled cheeks. A cowlick in his unruly dark hair.

She went through more pictures, finding one of the pair again in the cafeteria, another of them watching a baseball game, and another at their school desks during an exam of some sort.

Her excitement mounting, she returned to the graduate photos, this time searching for the mystery friend. Finally, she found him gazing back at her. *Donald Holtmeyer.*

"Did you know about Miss Bridget's brooch?" she whispered to the young man. "Do you know it's been under the living room floor in Michael and Miriam's house all these years? Are you the one who went into the house to polish it? Or was it somewhere else this whole time, and you just moved it there? Did you have anything to do with it at all?"

Reaching into her tote bag, she pulled out her phone, scrolled down to Liam's name in her contact list, and texted him. I THINK I FOUND A FRIEND OF MICHAEL SPENCER WHO MAY HAVE BEEN AROUND WHEN YOUR GRANDMOTHER'S BROOCH WENT MISSING.

Seconds later, a trio of dancing dots formed on the bottom corner of her screen, letting her know a reply was incoming. I'M ALL EARS. OR SHOULD I SAY EYES IN THIS CASE? ANYWAY, WHO WAS IT?

Chuckling, she texted back, DONALD HOLTMEYER. AND GET THIS—HE BELONGED TO A ROCKHOUND CLUB IN SCHOOL. IF HE WAS INTO ROCKS AND GEMS AS A TEEN, PERHAPS HE'S OUR MYSTERIOUS GEM POLISHER.

Again, she hit send. And, again, seconds later, more dancing dots followed.

HE CAN'T BE. HE PASSED AWAY DURING MY ROOKIE YEAR WITH THE DEPT. MAYBE ANOTHER FRIEND?

Shaking her head, she typed and sent her response. DH IS THE ONLY ONE I CAN FIND HANGING OUT WITH MICHAEL IN THE YEARBOOK. BACK TO SQUARE ONE, I GUESS.

GOOD SLEUTHING THOUGH.

"Not good enough," she murmured as she began to type. THANKS. WISH IT HAD LED SOMEWHERE. HAVE A GOOD REST OF YOUR DAY.

YOU TOO.

She deposited the phone into her bag and returned the yearbook to its shelf with far less enthusiasm than she'd retrieved it.

She'd been so sure the answer would be found with a friend of Michael Spencer—someone who'd known he'd taken the brooch and, for whatever reason, had felt compelled to…what? Keep it looking nice?

Sighing, she started toward the door but paused when her phone vibrated in her bag. Once again, she pulled it out, and felt her tension ease at the name displayed on the screen.

"Hey, Dad," she said as quietly as she could against a backdrop of giggles from the next room. "I'm in the library at the moment, so I can't talk any louder than this, and even *that's* probably breaking the rules."

"Any chance you could stop out here and see me before going into the restaurant today?" Dad asked.

Another voice rumbled in the background.

Her father sighed and amended his words. "See me *and* your uncle Gordon."

A third voice prompted a quiet groan directly into Hannah's ear. "I stand corrected. Again. See me, your uncle Gordon, and Bruce."

"Could we make it Sunday? After church?" she asked.

"Absolutely," her father said. "But I'd still like you to come today if possible. I have a little surprise for you."

Hannah glanced at her watch and then lifted her gaze to the window, which offered a view of the sign hanging above Jump Start Coffee nearby. It had taken all her willpower to wait on the coffee and Danish she'd envisioned upon waking that morning. Instead, she'd used the promise of it—and reading more of the journal she'd hastily added to her bag on the way out the door—as a carrot to visit the library and do some research.

And she had done that research. The fact her actions had led to nothing usable didn't negate her effort, did it?

"Hannah?"

"Sorry, Dad, I'm still here."

"So?" Dad asked. "Can you stop by?"

She pressed her free hand to her gurgling stomach. "I can be out there in about an hour if that works for you."

Her father's answering smile was practically audible through the phone. "It works perfectly, my dear. I'll—*we'll* see you then."

Chapter Eleven

She'd just pulled Miss Bridget's journal from her tote bag when Zane Forrest, the owner of Jump Start Coffee, appeared beside her table with a mug brimming with freshly roasted coffee in one hand and a cinnamon Danish in the other.

"One of the things I remember about you when we were growing up is the smile you always had whenever food was involved." He set the items on the table along with a napkin and utensils, arranging all neatly without spilling so much as a drop from the mug. "It was the same one you had a few minutes ago at the counter when you placed your order."

Closing her eyes, Hannah inhaled the coffee aroma, letting it chase away any residual tension from her fruitless trip to the library. "I've been dreaming about this coffee and this Danish all morning, and now the moment is *finally* here."

"But no pressure, of course," Zane joked.

"No pressure intended." She wrapped her fingers around the mug, lifted it for her first long-awaited sip, and set it back down with a contented sigh, relishing the flavor of the rich brew over her tongue. "I've been here before, remember? I know what your coffee tastes like, and I know what your Danish tastes like too. Which is why I've been dreaming about both all morning."

"I'm glad." He waited as she sampled a forkful of the pastry and then folded his arms across his chest. "I'm going to talk to him, you know. Ask him to give you another chance."

She took another bite and another sip. "Who?"

"Marshall Fredericks. The food critic."

"You saw the review."

Zane took the empty chair across from Hannah's. "I did. Jacob called me before he even finished reading it." The brothers shared many things in common. Working with food was just one of them.

"I'm sure you got quite an earful. He was pretty upset about it. We all were." Leaning forward, she wrapped both hands around the mug for comfort. "For what it's worth, your brother is fantastic at what he does. I'm so blessed that he came on as chef at the Hot Spot, and I'll always be grateful to you for recommending him to me."

"My pleasure, Hannah. I mean, I know he can forget who he's feeding sometimes with his over-the-top presentations, but the stuff he makes?" Zane gave a low whistle. "I can't deny his talent. No one can, as far as I'm concerned. Including Marshall Fredericks."

She took another long sip then chased it down quickly with another. "So, you know this food critic? Personally?"

Zane shrugged. "I know him well enough. He comes in here a few times a week on his way into the *Chronicle*. I don't necessarily always read his stuff in the paper—I probably would have missed his Hot Spot review if Jacob hadn't called me—but I make a point of checking his blog whenever I get a little free time."

She forked up another piece of her dessert. "Is his blog tied to the *Chronicle*?"

"No. It's something he does on his own, and it's starting to gain a real following, from what I can see. More and more people are commenting on his posts all the time."

Hannah popped the bite into her mouth. "What's it called?"

"*The Gourmet Guy.*"

She set her fork on her plate. "Seriously? I know that blog. In fact, it's one of the first places I go when I have to be on the internet for something."

Pushing her plate to the center of the table, she slumped back in her chair. "I can't believe the Gourmet Guy panned the Hot Spot. That makes what he had to say even worse."

"That doesn't mean he was right about your place," Zane said loyally. "Most people have no idea he's even behind the blog, and I get the sense he prefers it that way. I just found out from one of my baristas."

"It doesn't matter if anyone knows or not. His being the Gourmet Guy proves he knows his stuff. I've always found his posts to be insightful and spot-on. I can't think he's right about other stuff and wrong in his review of my place." She traced her finger around the rim of her mug. "Which means he must have been right."

Zane appraised her carefully. "So you weren't mad like Jacob was?"

She put her mug down. "I wanted that first-ever review to be glowing, of course. Who wouldn't? But he wasn't wrong."

"He didn't hate the actual food," Zane said. "Though I got the impression he wasn't thrilled with the presentation."

"Exactly. If he had problems with the food itself, *that* would've hurt us. But honestly? He might actually end up helping us, if I decide to take advantage of what he said." Hannah lifted her chin. "Which I'm doing."

"And Jacob? You think he'll listen and lay off the fancy prep stuff?"

"I think there'll have to be some compromise on both our parts, but yes, I do."

"It's your restaurant, Hannah," Zane reminded her.

"It is. And I hear what you're saying, Zane. But even before I came back to Blackberry Valley to open a restaurant, I knew I wanted to be a team with my staff. Which means I have to be willing to compromise too."

Zane slid off his chair and onto his feet. "My brother is a lucky guy to be working for you."

"And I'm lucky to have a chef as good as your brother in the kitchen of my restaurant."

He smiled and nodded at Miss Bridget's journal. "I know how hard it is to carve out any quiet time when you own a restaurant. So I'll leave you to yours for as long as you can stay. Enjoy the rest of your breakfast, Hannah. It's been nice chatting with you."

"You too, Zane. Thank you."

When he left, Hannah finished eating, being sure to wipe her hands well. She pushed her plate and mug away in favor of the journal, slowly ran her fingers down its leather cover, and finally flipped it open to the spot where she'd stopped reading two nights earlier.

November 16, 1963

Libby died today.

Patrick came to the library to tell me. My parents, my boss at the library, Pastor Lee—they had all said this day was coming. The increasing whispers at the market and the soda fountain agreed with them. I had plenty of warning. But I wanted to believe otherwise for Libby, for her husband, and most especially for Jerry.

That sweet child has brought me to tears with his whispered confidences more times than I can count since I first heard his sniffles all those months ago. I wiped his eyes and did my best to lift his spirits that day, but when he left, I knew he was returning to a reality I couldn't change for him, no matter how much I wished I could.

But then he came back the very next week. And the one after that. And the one after that. And every week after, including this one. He helped me to see how important kindness and empathy can truly be. I couldn't change Libby being sick, but I could be a steady hand, an encouraging voice, a loving hug, and a much-needed lifeline for her son. With me, he could cry, share his fears, and pray with a trusted adult he didn't have to worry about burdening further.

Today, though, I feel helpless again.

What do I say to a seven-year-old who lost his mother less than twenty-four hours after my most recent proclamation that everything would be okay? I pray that God will give me the right words when that time comes.

I'll stop writing now, so my tears won't smear the ink.

Death has a way of putting everything into perspective, doesn't it?

The next page in the journal featured a parade of exclamation points following the date, and Hannah smiled.

> *January 1, 1964!!!!!!!*
>
> *I am going to be Bridget Berthold!!!!!*
>
> *Patrick asked me to marry him on a magical walk this afternoon, during which I barely felt the cold. He got down on one knee, took my hand, and asked me right there in the middle of the park! For a moment I was too stunned to speak, but once I recovered my powers of speech, I imagine all of Blackberry Valley heard me say yes!*
>
> *I'm going to be Patrick's wife—Mrs. Patrick Berthold.*
>
> *I'm so excited, and so thankful to God for bringing this wonderfully sweet man into my life.*

At the end of the entry, Hannah allowed herself a moment to savor the joy in Miss Bridget's words. Nothing she'd read in the journal thus far lent itself to any sort of display at the Hot Spot. But seeing the lead-up to what she knew would soon become a behind-the-scenes look at the life of a firefighter's wife—well, that felt special.

"Hello, Hannah."

Turning to her right, she took in the fiftysomething man standing beside her table with a to-go cup in each hand and a tired smile on his pale, drawn face. "Hello, Tom. How are you? How's your mom?"

Tom Spencer grimaced. "I guess I thought being back in her own bed would help her sleep better, but that hasn't happened. In fact, I think she's actually sleeping worse."

"Any particular reason?" Hannah motioned for Tom to take the empty chair across from hers. "If the women from our church group need to take another go at the smell, we can. Maybe as soon as tomorrow, after the floor repairs are finished."

"Thank you for the offer." Tom set both cups on the table as he sat but kept his hands wrapped around them. "There's definitely still a smell, but I'm keeping the windows open whenever possible to let it air out."

"That should help quite a bit." Hannah closed Miss Bridget's journal to give him her full attention. "So when do you have to return to Cave City?"

Tom rubbed the stubble on his cheek. "I might actually stick around a little longer. See how things go."

"Meaning at your mom's place?" Hannah asked. "Because if you need to get back to your own life, I can assure you, your mom will be well looked after."

Tom shook his head. "I'm in no rush."

"You must have an understanding boss."

Tom snorted bitterly. "That's one word I never would've used to describe him, even before he laid me off three weeks ago."

"Oh, Tom, I'm so sorry to hear that. I didn't know."

"That's because I haven't even told my mother yet."

She reached across the table and briefly touched his hand. "I can't imagine the stress. First the job and then a fire at your mom's? You must be worn out."

"Maybe I should be. But all that's truly wearing me out is my mom. I don't know if I'm used to sleeping in silence after years of living alone, or if I'm afraid she's going to fall moving around late at night the way she does. Probably both." Tom picked up the cups and stood. "The fire itself isn't weighing on me at all. Not in a bad way, anyway."

She tilted her head at his words. "I don't understand."

"Depending on how much the insurance company gives us for damages and how much it will cost for the men at your church to fix everything, that fire may end up being more of a blessing than any sort of real tragedy. Especially now, in light of—" He stopped abruptly then motioned to the coffee shop's exit with both cups. "Anyway, I should get back to the house with these before they get cold, but I know Mom wants to hit up your new place for dinner, so I'm sure we'll see you soon."

"Looking forward to seeing you both." Hannah watched Tom cross to the door, a sense of unease creeping up her spine. She shoved her hand inside her tote bag, plucked out her phone, and scrolled through her contact list until she found the person most capable of setting her overactive imagination at ease.

"Good morning, Hannah!" came the familiar chipper voice.

"Good morning, Lacy." She checked her watch and then rested her cheek in her free hand. "Since it's nearly ten thirty, I imagine you're done feeding the animals."

"We are."

She smiled at the pronoun choice and the image it created in her mind's eye. "Neil took a day off from the bookstore? Though, as I'm saying that out loud, if he ever actually wanted to take his scheduled Monday off, I could fill in at the farm so the two of you could go hiking or work on one of your puzzles together or whatever."

"Neil's working at the store today, as usual. I would never ask you to do that on your own day off."

"You wouldn't be asking, Lacy. I'm volunteering. Because what else do I have to do on Mondays?"

"Sleep, take a walk, make yummy stuff to eat in your own kitchen, come do a puzzle with me, put yourself in a place to meet someone who'll sweep you off your feet and make it so you never leave Blackberry Valley ever again. Better yet, all of the above."

Amused, Hannah rolled her eyes to the coffee shop ceiling. "Real subtle, Lacy."

Her friend laughed. "You gotta admit, you pretty much eat, sleep, and breathe the Hot Spot."

Hannah sighed. "That's restaurant life, Lacy. It just is."

"I get that—to a point. But it's okay to take some time for yourself sometimes too. In fact, it's healthy."

"The Hot Spot *is* for me, Lacy. I've always wanted to own a restaurant, remember?"

"I remember. And you've made it happen."

"I got it off the ground, yes," Hannah said. "And we're feeding people five nights a week. But I'm sure you saw the review in the *Chronicle*. I still have a lot to do to get it where I want it."

"And you will." There wasn't an ounce of doubt in Lacy's tone. "Especially if you take a little time to do other things too. Breaks are necessary for your creativity, as well as for your health."

Hannah ran her hand down the front of the journal. "I was actually *trying* to do something else about an hour ago. But unfortunately, I came up empty-handed."

"Oh?"

"Yeah, I was at the library when it opened this morning."

"That sounds like you're taking a little time for yourself. I'm proud of you."

"I didn't go to the library to get a book. I went to do a little sleuthing."

"Ooh. Do tell."

Hannah settled back in her chair. "I couldn't let go of the two things: Michael Spencer is dead, and the brooch is freshly polished."

"The only thing we know from that is he couldn't have done the polishing, right?"

"Right. So I was wondering whether Michael had a close friend around the time the brooch was stolen."

"You think Michael's friend took it?" Lacy asked.

Hannah mulled that over while she carried her empty plate and cup to the designated spot for them at the counter. "I hadn't considered *that*, specifically. I wondered whether a friend might have known Michael stole it, and then the friend broke into Miriam's house and polished it."

"Interesting theory. But how does the library fit in?"

"Evangeline Cooke, the head librarian, said they have every one of Blackberry Valley High's yearbooks. I found Michael Spencer's graduating class and searched that yearbook for any sign of someone who might appear to be a good friend."

"And?"

"I found one." Hannah released a long breath. "But he too has passed away."

"Ugh. I really thought that might go somewhere, even though you said you came up empty-handed."

"I was hoping. But now I'm thinking maybe it wasn't a friend at all," Hannah said. "Maybe it was family."

"You lost me."

Hannah went back to her table and sat down again. "I just saw Tom Spencer a few minutes ago."

"He's still in town?"

"Yes. And… Listen, can I say something to you I probably shouldn't be thinking, much less saying?"

"Isn't that what best friends are for?"

"Don't mention this to anyone, but Tom lost his job. He hasn't even told Miriam yet, so it's probably best she doesn't find out from anyone else."

"That's awful. Poor guy."

"That happened three weeks ago," she said, lowering her voice. "*Before* the fire."

"Sometimes it doesn't rain," Lacy said. "It pours."

"Actually, he told me the fire isn't weighing on him at all." She let Lacy's answering silence linger for a moment before continuing. "He said, depending on the money they get from insurance, it could actually end up being a blessing. Especially now."

"Are you saying what I think you're saying?" Lacy asked.

"I don't want to be."

"Neil said there's still been no announcement on the cause of the fire yet."

Hannah thought back to the little bit of information that Liam had shared with her, and she swallowed. "There hasn't been. But if Tom was involved with that fire in any way, it'll break Miriam's heart."

"Agreed, but we weren't talking about the fire when you brought up Tom just now. We were talking about the brooch."

"Maybe he knew his father had stolen it and stashed it under the floor," Hannah said. "Maybe he's the one who polished it."

"I was there when you found it, remember? And I can assure you that Tom was every bit as surprised by that brooch being there as the rest of us were."

Hannah rubbed her temple. "Okay, so maybe tying him to the brooch is a bit of a stretch. But the fire? He *did* say that insurance thing."

"Sounds like you have reason to reach out to Liam again." Lacy's tone was a little too innocent.

"I don't know, Lacy. I had a hard enough time putting the question out to you, and you're my friend."

"Any reason Liam can't be your friend too?"

Hannah rolled her eyes. Lacy was hardly being subtle. "Of course not, but—"

"Oh, one second, Hannah. Mimi is trying to eat Penelope's shirt."

"Penelope, huh? That's the girl you called about last night, right? The one Dylan met at the coffee shop before the Hot Spot opened. You hired her?"

"I did. If she was good enough for Miriam, she'll be good enough for me. She started this morning."

"That's why you said 'we' earlier." Hannah slid the journal into her tote bag. "It's going okay so far?"

"So far, yes."

Hannah paused as she digested her friend's words. "Hey, what do we know about this girl, exactly? I mean, prior to working for

Miriam, where did she live? What did she do? Has she ever been in any trouble that we know of? Anything that—"

"Whoa. I know where you're going with this, Hannah, and it went through my head too. But from what I can tell, Penelope really needed the job at Miriam's. Starting a fire there would have been completely counterproductive for her."

"Maybe," Hannah admitted reluctantly.

"She's also still in Blackberry Valley, and she's not from here," Lacy continued. "If she set the fire for some unknown reason, why would she stick around? Wouldn't she take off?"

"Fine. I see what you're saying." Hannah drew in a breath and released it with a huff. "At least now you have a little help."

"Yes, and I'm already grateful for it."

"Does that mean you might actually be able to join me for breakfast at Jump Start Coffee sometime soon?"

Lacy laughed. "We'll see how it goes."

"That's not a no."

"You're right, it's not."

Pulling the strap of her tote bag up her arm, Hannah slid off the chair and onto her feet. "Tell Mimi that if she's a good girl and doesn't try to eat Penelope's shirt again, I'll give her a treat the next time I see her."

"Who're you kidding? You'll give Mimi a treat whether she's good or not."

It was Hannah's turn to laugh. "You're right. I will."

"Where are you off to now?" Lacy asked.

"My dad's. Apparently, he, Uncle Gordon, and a friend of theirs have a surprise for me."

"And you thought you knew everything there was to know about Blackberry Valley. I bet you never suspected you'd be mired in mysteries from the word go."

Hannah waved to Zane behind the counter and headed for the door. "I think the one about the ruby is enough. It wasn't as if I was bored before that."

"We're making sure that never happens," Lacy replied. "Between the ruby and the fire, whether they're connected or not."

"And I'd appreciate that more if I felt as if I were getting anywhere with either mystery," Hannah told her friend. "Unfortunately, I don't feel as if I know anything more than I did when we first found the brooch."

Chapter Twelve

Hannah parked beside a tan-colored sedan she didn't recognize, cut the engine, and took a moment to soak in the vibrant colors of the petunias, creeping zinnia, and purple coneflowers that lined the walkway to her childhood home.

There was so much about the view of the house from the driveway that always flooded her with memories of her mom—the porch swing where they'd sat together and talked about everything, the window of the bedroom they'd painted the year she turned thirteen, the screen door her mother called through when Hannah got off the school bus each day, and the assorted flower beds in front of her now. So many of the bushes and plants were ones she and her mom planted together.

Before everything changed.

Even now, eight years later, she still felt the pain of her mother's death as strongly as if it had just happened. But she also felt her mother's presence. She'd sensed her encouraging push when it was time for her to return to her job and her life in California, and she'd sensed the reassurance of her arms on the many nights she'd cried herself to sleep after. When the time was right to finally move back home for good, she'd imagined her mother's hand in hers every step of the way. And when she'd cut the ceremonial new-business ribbon outside the Hot Spot on opening day, her mind's eye had allowed her mother to be there, standing right next to her dad and wiping tears of joy from her eyes.

"I feel you with me, Mom," she whispered. "Every single day. Everywhere, but especially here."

Blinking back the tears that had begun to blur the flowers, Hannah raised her head to see her father standing on the front porch, his gentle smile telling her that he knew what she'd been thinking because he felt the same way.

She waved, dropped her keys into her bag, and climbed out of her car and onto the gravel driveway.

He met her on the sidewalk with a kiss on her forehead. "I'm glad you're here, sweetheart."

"I am too, Dad." She took a deep breath of fresh air scented with her mother's blooms. "Mom would love this year's flowers."

He pulled her in for a hug then cleared his throat as he released her. "And the fact that I used her recipe for the cookies I just took out of the oven."

Hannah stared at him. "Mom's oatmeal scotchies?"

"As if I could welcome you home with anything else."

Leaning forward, she kissed his cheek. "Dad, you're the best. Thank you."

"Hold your thanks until we see whether I destroyed them or not," Dad said, grinning. "I've never claimed to be a great baker."

"I'm grateful for the gesture no matter how they taste."

The telltale creak of the screen door being opened again was quickly drowned out by the sound of a happy bark. Hannah crouched down and opened her arms to greet her father's border terrier, who dashed toward her and covered her face in doggy kisses.

"Okay, okay, Zeus. Enough," Dad said. "Hannah is here to see me, boy. *Me*."

"*And* me."

Hannah straightened, smiling at her uncle, who stood next to her father. "Hi, Uncle Gordon. I hear cookies have been made."

"They have." Uncle Gordon wrapped Hannah in a bear hug. "I was threatened with no dinner if I ate one before your arrival."

Hannah slanted her attention back onto her father. "A valid threat when it comes to Mom's oatmeal scotchies. No one can eat just one."

The three of them laughed before Uncle Gordon swept his hand toward the front porch. "Your father didn't threaten Bruce, so we might want to hurry up and go inside."

"Zeus, why are you not inside standing guard?" Hannah teased.

"Because nothing is more important to him than you are, my dear," her father said, falling in step with her as they followed Uncle Gordon to the house.

"Except a dog biscuit, a tennis ball, or your lap," Hannah replied, laughing.

Uncle Gordon held the screen door open for Hannah. "Or his new squeaky toy. Right, Zeus?"

Zeus darted around Hannah into the hallway, his tail wagging. "I know, boy. Dad used to spoil me like that too."

Where the hallway came to a T with the living room to the left and the kitchen to the right, Hannah followed the smell of the cookies as her eyes grew misty. "They smell just like they're supposed to, Dad."

"I'll take that as an encouraging sign." Dad directed Hannah to the table as he headed for the counter and the plate of cookies. Uncle Gordon retrieved a pitcher of iced tea from the refrigerator.

Hannah took in the place setting for four as Bruce came in from the sunporch. "Hello, Bruce, we meet again."

"With cookies this time." Bruce patted her arm, grimacing slightly as he did. "It's good to see you, Hannah. I thoroughly enjoyed my dinner at your restaurant the other night."

"And we enjoyed having you." She ushered him to one of the chairs at the table and then sat beside him. Her uncle poured tea into the four waiting glasses while her father set the plate of cookies in the center of the table. "Oh, Dad, they look as good as they smell."

Dad and Uncle Gordon took their seats. "Now for the real test," her father said, motioning for her to try one.

Hannah selected a cookie and pinched off a bite. It melted in her mouth, as her mother's had always done. "Wow, Dad. These are incredible. Mom would be so proud."

Eyes glistening, Dad managed a smile. "Thank you, Hannah."

"No, thank *you*, Dad." She grinned at her uncle. "When did Dad become a baker?"

Uncle Gordon chuckled. "When you told him you'd come by today."

"And what? He found Mom's recipe in her recipe box and made *these*, just like that?"

"That's right," Uncle Gordon said.

Hannah took another cookie from the plate. "Keep it up and I might have to put you to work at the Hot Spot, Dad. I'm sure Jacob wouldn't mind a pastry chef."

"Zeus would never forgive me, would you, boy?" Dad asked, looking down at the dog who leaned against his leg. "But I'll make these cookies every time you visit if that'll have you out here more often."

She lifted her glass of iced tea in a toast. "Deal. Though I don't need an incentive to come out here. I just need time."

"From what I've heard, that isn't an easy thing to find when you're in the restaurant business," Bruce said as he too helped himself to a second cookie.

She took a sip of her drink then said, "The restaurant business can be all-consuming. For years when I lived in California, my days were literally just work and sleep. But it was all I ever wanted to do, and it was a means to an end—owning my own place."

"The best restaurant in Blackberry Valley," Dad said proudly. "Maybe all of Kentucky."

Uncle Gordon broke a third cookie in half and handed a piece to Bruce. "Being closed on Sundays and Mondays should help in terms of having a life outside of the Hot Spot, right?"

"Someday, yes. But for now, the Hot Spot is still new," Hannah said. "That means I spend my 'free time' getting the word out—trying to convince publications to write a story, figuring out the best places to run ads, building a social-media following, and keeping up on customer reviews."

"That does sound like a lot," Bruce said.

"Then, because we're a farm-to-table restaurant, I also research and order from local farms, work with Jacob on the menu, and make sure we always have whatever supplies we need," Hannah continued. "There are also managerial tasks like scheduling, training, and making sure to reward staff for various benchmarks. Oh, and since our first critical review, I need to make a serious push to amp up the firehouse theme. Which, thanks to the Berthold family, is a bit less daunting because now I don't have to figure out how to make the history more personable. On the other hand, figuring out how and where to display everything is a whole different story."

The three men exchanged smiles.

"What was that about?" she asked.

"What was what about?" Her uncle looked at her innocently.

She folded her arms over her chest as she took in Bruce's rounded eyes, her uncle's sudden need to rearrange his napkin just so, and her father's sheepish expression. "Well, first of all, Dad insisted that I come out today. And now you three are acting weird."

"You like the cookies, don't you?" her father asked.

Hannah narrowed her eyes at him. "Yes. Very much. But that doesn't change the fact that something's up."

Uncle Gordon chuckled. "Tell her, Gabriel."

"I don't know where to start," Dad protested.

Uncle Gordon rolled his eyes. "Maybe the beginning. Dinner the other night."

Hannah scooted to the edge of her seat. "It was all right, wasn't it? If you had any problems, I need to know right away."

Her dad patted her hand. "It was perfect, as usual. But the three of us got to thinking about that box of memorabilia the fire chief gave you that evening."

Hannah smiled. "I told you about the picture or two I saw that night, but I've gotten to look at everything else since then. I'll need to buy a lot of frames, that's for sure. Everything is incredible."

"You also told us about the Blackberry Valley Fire Department patches they gave you," Dad said. "You mentioned how neat it was that they show the changes in the design over the years. Gordon, will you grab it?"

Uncle Gordon ducked out of the room then returned with a wooden box in one hand and a milk crate in the other. "Here it is. Go on, Gabriel."

"We all thought that the difference in patches through the years could be a really interesting thing for your customers to see as well, so we thought you might like a way to highlight that. We went to work on a display case. Bruce came up with the design, your uncle constructed it and found the right glass, and I wired in some lighting. Show her, Gordon."

Still holding the milk crate under one arm, Uncle Gordon carefully handed the wooden box to Hannah. "When we started talking about this on the way home from your restaurant, I envisioned all the patches lined up in a case like this. Bruce thought it would be neat to have them side by side, with no partitions in between, so people could really take in the changes from one patch to the other. So I tried it that way, and I think he's right. I'm pretty sure you could put the extra badges in here too."

Pulling in a quick breath, Hannah soaked up every detail of the handcrafted display case, imagining it filled with the patches from Liam and his grandfather, plus the one Liam said his father would send in the mail. "This is *gorgeous*. Absolutely gorgeous. I can't believe you made this for me, and so quickly."

"We're just some retired old guys with far too much time on our hands," Uncle Gordon said, laughing.

She set the case on the table and ran her hand along the smooth, beveled wooden trim around the outside of the glass. "Uncle Gordon,

I know you were a plumber by trade and that you also worked with glass, but I didn't know you could build like this."

"I had a skilled coach." Her uncle nodded to Bruce.

"You helped build this?" she asked him.

Bruce showed her fingers gnarled and crooked with age. "I wish. But in an ironic twist of fate, I—the guy who spent his whole career building things—have arthritis, so my hands can no longer be counted on for detailed work of any kind."

"Bruce is far too humble, Hannah. Like I said, he designed it," Dad hastily interjected. "Gordon and I simply implemented his plan."

With obvious effort, Bruce maneuvered his fingers around his glass. "Which means the reason you actually have a display case now is because of your dad and your uncle. If it were up to me alone, you'd merely have the idea."

"Well, I appreciate all of your contributions." Again, she fingered the wood trim as she peered in at the place where the badges would be displayed. "I don't know what to say. The idea, the design, the craftsmanship, the lighting—it's all perfect. Thank you, Dad. Thank you, Uncle Gordon. And thank you, Bruce. I can't wait to get this hung up inside the Hot Spot."

"I'm glad you like it, sweetheart," Dad said. "But there's more."

Chapter Thirteen

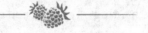

"But, Dad, you've already done so much for me," Hannah protested when she found her voice again. "I don't need anything else."

Dad waved away her concerns. "The case is something to aid in displaying what you got from the fire chief. And we enjoyed making it. But we wanted to take a swipe at that food critic too."

"Marshall Fredericks didn't do anything wrong. He really didn't. In fact, what he wrote opened my eyes to ways I can make the Hot Spot even better, and I'm good with that. Grateful, actually. I mean, I was hoping my first review would be five stars in every category, of course. Who wouldn't? But when the Hot Spot is finally worthy of such a review, I want it to be because I made it so. And it's clear to me that I haven't—yet."

"Everything we had was delicious," Dad argued. "Right, guys?"

The men nodded.

"He didn't ding us on the food. He simply felt swirls on the plate were a little much for a particular menu item and, frankly, I have to agree." She took another sip of her iced tea. "I do wish I'd put more thought into playing up the firehouse theme. That writer made me stop and view things from a customer's perspective. Now I'm not only going to play it up, I'm also going to give it a real hometown feel. The theme won't simply be firehouse, it'll be *Blackberry Valley's* firehouse and its history in this town."

"That'll build more of a connection with the locals," Bruce said.

"Which is my goal." Hannah squeezed her father's arm. "So I really do believe Marshall Fredericks helped me out."

Dad gazed at her in silence for a moment before a broad smile broke over his face. "Your mother would be so proud of you, Hannah. So proud of the hardworking, positive-minded young woman you are. I know I am."

"Thanks, Dad."

"We still have something else for you." Dad gestured to her uncle. "Show her, Gordon."

Hannah's uncle reached into the milk crate and pulled out an object.

"Is that a bell?" she asked.

"It is." Her father abandoned his spot at the table to stand next to her uncle. "From the fire station you now own. It used to hang right outside the front door."

She gaped at it. "How did you get this?"

"I did some work for the Blackberry Valley Fire Department back in the day. Once they asked me to replace the old bell with a light, and then they offered to let me keep the bell. I, of course, promptly shoved it into the garage never to be seen or thought of again, until yesterday when we were working on the case. Suddenly, it hit me like a ton of bricks that this would be perfect for the Hot Spot. The next thing I knew, I was pulling everything out of the garage to find it."

"Oh, Dad, you're right, this is perfect!"

Uncle Gordon motioned toward the bell. "Maybe you could ring it every day when you open."

"If the powers that be in Blackberry Valley don't mind, I think that would be a fun thing to do. Or at least for special occasions." She beamed at the three men. "Thank you so much for everything. The care, the effort, the thoughtfulness, the support—all of it. You've provided yet another reminder how glad I am that I returned home to turn my dream of opening my own restaurant into a reality."

"And how glad we are you did, sweetheart." Dad brushed a kiss across Hannah's temple while her uncle set the bell back inside the milk crate.

She stood and put the display on top of the milk crate. "Unfortunately, as much as I'd love to stay and visit longer, I do need to head out. Friday and Saturday are our busiest nights at the Hot Spot, and I want to be ready."

"We understand." Dad stopped her from lifting the crate and case. "Why don't you go ahead and take the display case now, but leave the bell? I'll come hang it up either Sunday after church or sometime Monday. Whichever works best for you."

"That'd be great, thanks." She hurried around the table, pecking each of the three men on the cheek. "Thank you again. I'm beyond excited to get this display case up on the wall. It's positively beautiful."

"I really didn't do anything," Bruce protested, blushing.

She gently squeezed his shoulder. "Oh yes, you did. Your design is beautiful, and I can't wait to show it off. It's a real masterpiece. Which means the three of you need to come back for dinner once I have it up on the wall."

"You won't get any argument from me," Uncle Gordon said.

She glanced at Bruce. "You'll come too, right?"

Bruce nodded, displaying a shy smile.

"Good."

Her father picked up the display case, and he and Zeus walked Hannah out to her car. Dad placed the case on the floor of her back seat and shut the door.

"Would you like to come over for lunch after church on Sunday?" Hannah asked him. "Or for dinner on Monday if you're free? I could make you something special as my way of saying thank you for the case and the bell and the cookies."

"The joy on your face is all the thanks I need, Hannah."

"If you say so, but I make a mean pasta salad," she teased.

Her father laughed. "If it means more time with you, I'll see what I can do."

She paused with her hand on the handle of the car door. "I know the anniversary of Mom's death is coming up. Are you okay?"

"I am. My long walks with Zeus and volunteer work up at the church keep me busy. And I like puttering around with Gordon and Bruce." Dad smiled at her. "Thank you for being so generous in your praise for Bruce. For someone whose livelihood depended on his hands, the limited use of them now has been quite a struggle for him."

"My praise was sincere." She climbed behind the steering wheel, took her keys from her tote bag, and then rested them on her lap. "Can I ask you something?"

"Of course."

"Do you know anything about Miriam's son, Tom?"

Dad pulled back, surprised. "Are you interested in him? I would have thought he might be a bit old for you."

She chuckled. "Dating-wise? No. I'm way too busy with the restaurant to even consider the notion of dating."

"For now, maybe," Dad countered. "But things should settle down enough that you can soon, right?"

She laughed. "Maybe one day. I don't have the bandwidth to even think about trying to meet someone new."

"It doesn't have to be someone new, Hannah. It could be someone you've already met—someone you're getting to know right now because of what that critic wrote."

She frowned in confusion before she put the pieces together. "Wait. You're not talking about Liam Berthold, are you?"

"He's well respected in Blackberry Valley. He comes from a good, solid family. And I like the way he's being so thoughtful toward you. Your mother would like that too."

"He's a nice guy. That's all."

"Friendship is a good place to start."

She held up her hands. "I'm not trying to start anything right now. The timing isn't right."

"I'm sorry. I don't mean to pry. I was just so happy with your mother, and I want that kind of happiness for you someday." Dad leaned against her open car door as Zeus sniffed around his feet, her feet, the interior of the car, and the gravel beneath it all. "As for what I know about Tom Spencer, it's not a lot. I know he doesn't live in Blackberry Valley anymore, but I'm guessing he lives pretty close, since I see him with Miriam a lot."

"He lives in Cave City."

"Then I was right. I know he's been involved in a lot of different enterprises.

"What do you mean?"

Her father hemmed and hawed, as if trying to figure out a polite way to say something unpleasant. Finally, he landed on, "Get-rich-quick kind of things that often had him hitting up his mother's friends to buy this or try that. But not recently, as far as I know. I assumed he mended his ways some time ago."

She let out a long, labored sigh. "I was hoping you'd have something that would settle my mind about him, not make me feel worse."

"Why?" Dad asked, peering into her face. "What's going on? Is this because you were helping out at his mom's the other day? And now he feels he knows you enough to try and bring you in on one of his schemes?"

"No." She sighed again. "Please keep this between us, but I'm starting to wonder if he may have had a hand in the fire. For insurance purposes. And I don't know what to do with that. Do I confront him? Do I share my suspicions with Liam or Sheriff Steele? I don't want to spread unfounded suspicions, but I also don't want anyone to get away with arson."

Her father squeezed her hand. "Put it out of your mind, Hannah. The fire was ruled accidental."

"When was that?" she asked, startled. "I spoke with Liam about this last night, and he made it sound like it's very much an active investigation."

"At that time, maybe it was. But on today's morning news it was officially ruled an accident. It seems to have been started by a makeup mirror that happened to be turned in such a way that the sun's reflection caught the curtains on the other side of the room on fire. Hence the difficulty in determining the cause those first few days."

She stared at her father. "A makeup mirror? Seriously? I've never heard of such a thing."

"Apparently, it's rare, but not impossible."

"A makeup mirror," she said again before resting her head back against her seat. "Well, I guess that's better than what my brain was dreaming up. Now I don't have to risk upsetting Miriam with questions about her son and I can focus my attention on figuring out who stole the ruby brooch and kept it hidden all these years."

Her dad chuckled. "I take it you've found your way to the mystery section of Legend & Key Bookstore."

"Huh?"

"I'm glad you're finding time to read amidst all the stress of the restaurant," Dad went on. "That's good. But make sure to get outside some too. In fact, maybe Zeus and I can come into town and go for a walk with you once in a while." He rubbed the border terrier's head and then picked him up. "That would be great, wouldn't it, Zeus? You, me, and Hannah going for a walk in the park?"

Zeus wriggled his whole body in response, as if he understood what was on offer.

Hannah laughed. "Sure, we can go for a walk sometime. Maybe even on Sunday if we do lunch together. But I don't get how we got from what I said to Neil's bookstore." She shot straight up in her seat. "Wait. I didn't tell you about the brooch I found, did I?"

"No. I thought you were talking about a mystery novel you're reading. You mean you found a brooch in real life?"

So she filled him in on it. About finding the compartment under the floorboard of Miriam's living room containing the heavy dust and the squashed paper and the freshly polished brooch. About learning from Miss Bridget's journal that the brooch had been stolen in 1963. About Michael Spencer's crush on Miss Bridget when she dated Liam's grandfather. About Hannah's suspicions that Michael had stolen the brooch and hidden it under the floor and that perhaps a friend of his had known and recently polished it. About finding a possible lead on a friend in the old yearbook but realizing she'd reached a dead end at the news of the friend's passing a few years before.

When she was done, she looked at her dad and waited.

"Wow." He rested his chin on top of Zeus's head. "That's…a lot."

"I know."

"And the paper?" Dad asked. "Anything special about it?"

Surprised, she said, "Paper? You mean the flyer that was in the box with the brooch?"

"Yes."

"I didn't look at it all that closely before Tom threw it away. It was an advertisement for some place called Dave's that sold what seemed to be classic cars."

Dad's eyebrow lifted. "Dave's?"

"You know the place?" she asked.

"I do. Or should say, *did*. The cars sold there would indeed be considered classic today. They were new when Dave was selling them."

"I don't understand."

"Dave's was on Hanley Road. It's where my father bought the car I remember riding in as a kid, a blue 1966 Chevy Impala. Gordon and I were with Dad when he bought it, and I think I was about five or six. Dave himself came out to where we were waiting and gave us both suckers. Mine was red, and Gordon's was green. They were good."

She laughed. "They must've been if you still remember them."

"I'm really remembering Dave. He was a nice man. Died of a heart attack about six months later."

Her smile faded. "I'm sorry to hear that."

"You know the gas station on the corner of Hanley and Market? That's where Dave's was back then." Dad waved his hand. "Anyway, if you're right, and the brooch was, at some point, wrapped in an old Dave's ad, I think it's safe to say the brooch was there a long time."

"That, and the dust," she murmured. "Regardless, though, I'm back to square one."

"On something you can and *should* let the sheriff's department deal with," Dad pointed out.

"I know, and normally I would. But since the brooch has been recovered, I've gotten the impression that the sheriff's department doesn't intend to investigate it. Liam and his grandfather have been so kind to me, and if I can repay them by figuring out who stole the brooch all those years ago and why, I'd like to do that. Plus, seeing as how I'm the one who found it, I'd kind of like to know how it got there, you know?"

Her father chuckled. "You and your mother always did love reading your horse stories and your mysteries."

She shrugged. "This is more than that. Honestly. It's impacting people I know and care about. I always loved Miss Bridget. You know that."

"I do." He gave her one last hug and stepped away from the car. "But I also know you're asking a lot of yourself with the restaurant right now. So don't run yourself into the ground over this, okay?"

"I won't. I promise."

He waited until she started the engine, and then closed the door, smiling at her through the open window. "I'll see you at church on Sunday?"

"Absolutely. And then sometime after that, you'll come to my place for some pasta salad?"

"And to hang the bell over the Hot Spot's door," he added. "I can also hang the display case, if it's ready to go up. And anything else you might want on the wall."

"Thanks, Dad. I really appreciate that. It's going to be so perfect."

"It's good having you back home, kiddo. It really is."

"I couldn't agree more. Thanks for everything. You really do spoil me."

His laugh hovered in the air as he held on to Zeus so she could exit the driveway. "My pleasure, Hannah. Have a great night at work. And because I know you too well to think you're going to let this go, I suppose I should also wish you happy sleuthing."

Chapter Fourteen

As Hannah drove, she called Jacob. She had another stop to make and wanted to let him know she might be later than usual.

Her chef picked up on the first ring. "Hi, Hannah." In the background of the call, Hannah could hear the usual sounds of a busy kitchen.

"You're at the Hot Spot already?" she asked. "We don't open for hours yet."

"I'm at home, actually." She heard a quick stirring and, seconds later, a cabinet closing before he went on. "I'm trying out a new seasonal recipe we might want to put on the menu. Something *without* swirls, in case you're wondering."

She chuckled. "I wasn't. And I look forward to trying what you've come up with because I know it will be divine. It always is."

"You say that, yet you still push back when it comes to including some of those things on the menu," Jacob said as the stirring resumed.

"Because some of what you come up with is more like what you'd find in a high-end restaurant like the ones I worked at in California. The Hot Spot isn't like that."

What sounded like the whack of a spoon against a skillet was followed by, "But it *could* be."

"We're housed in an old firehouse, Jacob."

"That doesn't mean anything," he grumbled.

"We're housed in an old firehouse in *Blackberry Valley, Kentucky*," she said. "Which means we should be a place *everyone* can enjoy." Reminding herself that she and her staff were a team, she added, "But we can give some thought to including one or two more high-end seasonal dishes throughout the year. We can discuss that if you'd like."

"How about two or three? That way we can have a high-end option for various palates and dietary restrictions."

She saw a car approaching in her sideview mirror and made the decision to turn left rather than going straight toward Blackberry Valley's small yet well-appointed downtown. "We'll talk about it at our staff meeting on Tuesday."

"I would appreciate that. Thank you."

"It's not a guarantee. But I'll keep an open mind."

She heard the skillet being set down followed by the sound of running water. "Is that why you called?" he asked.

Hannah made a right at a stop sign. "No, but I'm glad we talked about it. I was calling to let you know that it might be closer to two thirty before I'm at the restaurant today. I want to stop at Miriam Spencer's place and see how she's doing."

"Did you hear what started the fire?" Jacob asked. "It was a mirror, of all things. Can you believe it?"

She slowed as she approached the mailbox marked SPENCER and then started up the long driveway. She wound her way past trees and shrubs until her elderly friend's small but attractive home sprang into view. "A makeup mirror, from what my dad said."

"I think that's right. I'd just gotten in and flipped on the TV for some background noise when I heard the reporter talking to the fire chief. Once I heard it was accidental and something about a mirror, I turned my attention back to what I wanted to do in the kitchen."

After pulling to a stop in front of the house, Hannah shifted into park. "Anyway, I'm at Miriam's house now, so I need to go. But I'll be in as soon as I can."

"No problem, boss. I'll see you then." He clicked off.

She popped her key fob into her bag and stepped onto the dirt driveway. Immediately, the acrid scent of smoke met her nose, a reminder of what had transpired in the house the previous week.

"Why, Hannah! What a nice surprise." Miriam waved to her from the front porch.

"Hi, Miriam." Hannah hurried up the walkway lined with carefully tended flower beds. "I was on my way back to town from my dad's house and thought I'd take a moment to stop by and see how you're doing."

"How kind of you, dear." Miriam stopped her rocker with her sandaled toe and waved Hannah to the empty one on her left. "Come sit with me. How have you been?"

She set her bag on the ground beside the empty chair and sat. "I'm doing well. Busy, but that's par for the course in my profession. Not being busy would be far worse. I hear you're not sleeping very well."

Miriam's welcoming smile melted into a scowl. "You've been speaking with my son, I see."

"He's concerned about you. You've been through a lot. Though I imagine finally having the fire ruled an accident must be a relief—for both you and Tom."

Miriam nodded. "He was on the phone with the insurance company the moment we got the news from Liam."

"Maybe you'll sleep better now with that worry off your plate," Hannah suggested.

"Or maybe Tom's boss will rethink letting my son go and things can get back to normal for both of us," Miriam groused. "Meaning him in his house, and me in mine."

"So he told you about losing his job?"

"He told me over lunch a little while ago." Miriam waved a hand. "Though why all the secrecy, I don't know."

"Tom was probably worried about the stress you've been under with the fire and about you being alone in its aftermath. He was probably trying to avoid adding to your concerns," Hannah pointed out. "He wants to help you, Miriam. Especially while he's out of work and has the opportunity."

"I had someone for that, dear. Someone who needed the work, understood what I needed and when, and seemed to really *want* to hear my stories, especially from back when I was a young twenty-something like her, starting out in this house. Tom lets me talk, but I can tell he's simply humoring me."

"You're talking about Penelope, right?"

Miriam's eyes lit up. "Yes, Penelope McIntosh. You know her?"

"Not personally. But I know she started out at Lacy's farm this morning."

Miriam stopped rocking. "She found work?"

"She did. From what I understand, she showed up at the farm asking for employment and Lacy decided to give her a shot. I take it Lacy didn't call you for a reference?"

"No."

Hannah shrugged. "She probably didn't want to bother you with everything you've had going on."

Miriam threw up her hands. "For heaven's sake. I had a fire that started in my guest room and caused fixable damage. I had a group of wonderful friends who descended on my house and got it to where I can at least stay here. I really don't have all that much 'going on,' as you say. I'm tired of people treating me like a fragile old woman." Miriam released a breath. "But, for what it's worth, had Lacy asked me for a recommendation, I'd have given a glowing one for Penelope. She's a hard worker."

"What kind of things did you have her doing?" Hannah asked.

"Cleaning, weeding, shopping, and just being a companion."

Hannah laid a hand over her friend's. "If you're ever feeling lonely, I can think of a handful of people—including me—who would love to come out here and spend time with you."

"And I'm sure you're right, dear. But with Penelope, it happened so naturally. She came up with insightful questions that got me talking about Michael, our wedding, buying this house, and raising Tom." Miriam rested her elbows on the armrests of her rocker and tented her fingers beneath her chin. "So many of my friends already know my stories, much like Tom. Penelope was a fresh audience. I'd hoped she could wait to find another job until the house was back to normal and Tom headed home, so she could come work for me again, but I know she needed the money."

Hannah reached across the open space between their chairs and rested her hand next to Miriam's elbow. "I'd be happy to take you out to the farm sometime to visit with her if you'd like."

Miriam beamed. "I'd like that very much, dear. If and when you have time, of course."

"I'll find a way to make the time. Soon."

The elderly woman patted Hannah's lingering hand. "Thank you."

Hannah started to rise but stopped. "You know now that the brooch we found under your living room floorboard on Tuesday evening belonged to Bridget Berthold, correct?"

The sparkle went out of Miriam's eyes. "I was told that, yes."

"And that it was stolen from her shortly after she received it?" Hannah added. "Did you know Miss Bridget back then?"

"I did," Miriam said, her lips drawing tight.

Hannah took a moment to compose her thoughts and then asked the question she couldn't ignore. "Were you friends?"

Miriam's answering laugh was bitter. "I knew of her, but we weren't what you'd call friends. She was a year or so younger than I was."

"Did your husband know her?" Hannah asked, ignoring the feeling that she was pressing her luck.

Miriam gave her a sharp look. "Why are you asking me that?"

Hannah swallowed. "Because I'm trying to figure out how her brooch ended up under the floor of your home."

Miriam stopped her rocker and got to her feet. "Don't forget it was freshly polished."

Hannah stood too, the relaxed atmosphere between them gone. "Of course. I know that. I was just—"

"I'm sorry, but I'm feeling very fatigued right now. Perhaps a need for that sleep Tom says I'm not getting has finally caught up with me." Miriam shuffled past her, pulled open the screen door, and glanced back. "Michael was a good man—a good man I saw, and who finally saw me too. I won't let you or anyone else in this town tarnish his reputation."

"I'm not trying to do that," Hannah assured her. "I'm merely trying to figure out what happened all those years ago."

"Why? Haven't the police turned the brooch over to Patrick?"

"I don't know, but I imagine they will soon if they haven't," Hannah replied.

"Then what's the problem? It's back with the family again." Miriam went inside the house and spoke through the screen door. "Isn't that what matters?"

"Not to me. It was stolen and hidden under your floor over sixty years ago. Don't you want to know why? And don't you want to know who came into your house when you weren't around, and polished the brooch—without your knowledge or permission?"

"I have no explanation for that," Miriam murmured.

"You've said that. But that's what I'm trying to figure out. For the Berthold family, and for you."

Miriam stilled her hand on the edge of the interior wooden door. "We bought this house after our wedding in the fall of 1966."

Tilting her head, Hannah quickly did the math. "So three years after the brooch went missing."

Miriam met her gaze, her usually merry eyes cold. "Which means it would've already been there, under the floor, *before* we moved in."

"Not necessarily," Hannah mused. "There could've been a delay between it going missing and it being hidden. We don't know when it was placed under the floorboard."

"Well, good luck with that." With a single push of the door, Miriam brought an end to the conversation and the visit.

Chapter Fifteen

Hannah thanked six Blackberry Valley town council members for coming to the Hot Spot then glanced toward the kitchen. Her wide-eyed chef beckoned to her through the porthole-style window in one of the swinging doors.

She hurried across the dining room floor, nodding and smiling at each patron who made eye contact along the way.

"What did I not order enough of?" she asked as she entered the kitchen, scanning the room.

"Nothing." Jacob ushered her back to the door and pointed at the window. "I just wanted you to see. So you know."

Confused, she frowned at her chef. "See what? What are you talking about?"

"It's *him*."

She followed his finger back out to the dining area and the tables of people talking, laughing, and eating. "Can you be more specific, please?"

"At table four."

Hannah peered through the glass and spotted a young Black man with stylish glasses, and a wide smile directed at his attentive server, Raquel.

"Okay. I see him. Is there a reason you called me in here to point him out?"

"It's *him*," Jacob said again.

"What's the problem?" Hannah asked as she took in the young man, who was now laughing at something Raquel was saying. "He looks like a nice guy."

Jacob grunted. "He's not."

"How do you know him?"

"We *both* do, Hannah."

She raised an eyebrow at her chef. "I don't know that guy. I've never seen him before."

"Oh, but you know him. It's Marshall Fredericks."

Her gaze shot back to the man. "Marshall Fredericks? He's here *again*?"

Jacob snorted. "Of course he is. My food is fantastic, and he knows it."

She examined the table in front of the reviewer, noting the full glass of water, the fresh napkin, the absence of a plate or utensils, and an open book beside him. "I think he's ordered a dessert. But did he eat dinner too?"

"I don't know, but I'll check." Jacob hurried over to the stack of finished order sheets in a basket beside the grill, fished through them, and then held one up. "He had the Rookie Meltdown with pepper jack cheese and a side order of fries."

"Do you know if you swirled anything on the plate?" she asked, suddenly breathless.

Jacob propped his hands on his apron-clad hips. "There's nothing to swirl on a Rookie Meltdown."

"As if that's ever stopped you," Hannah pointed out.

"I think I'm offended. Or I would be if you weren't right. I just like the plates to look like some effort went into them."

"I know. Should I go out and welcome him? Pretend I don't know who he is? Oh my goodness. Here comes Raquel."

Hannah stepped back to allow the server into the kitchen. When the door swung closed, Hannah grabbed her hand. "The guy at table four. Do you know who that is?"

"It took me a second to recognize him. He isn't wearing his glasses in his profile picture. But now that I've seen him in them, I think he should have a new photo taken with them."

Raquel grabbed a tub of homemade vanilla ice cream from the stainless-steel freezer then crossed to the shelf of pies. "But yes, I know who he is. He's even more adorable in person, isn't he?"

Hannah followed her. "Did he mention whether he liked his Rookie Meltdown? Does he need anything else?"

"He loved it, and I'm being sure to take good care of him." Raquel calmly plated a piece of apple pie and topped it with a scoop of ice cream. "His face positively lit up when I asked if he wanted his apple pie à la mode, so I get the sense he likes ice cream. Which is good, because our ice cream is the best." Raquel winked at Hannah as she added a second scoop.

"Obviously that means he should get extra without approval," Jacob grumbled.

Hannah nodded vigorously. "Oh, I approve. Absolutely. If he likes ice cream, give the man ice cream. Maybe it'll sweeten his opinion of us. I wish I'd known he was coming back so I could have had the memorabilia from Liam's family up on the walls."

Raquel grinned. "And when, exactly, would you have done that?"

"I mean, do I really need to sleep?"

Raquel laughed and left the kitchen with Marshall's pie, leaving Hannah with her chef.

Jacob resumed filling orders. "We shouldn't treat him differently. You know how food critics are. The likelihood he'll write another review on us is slim to none."

Hannah folded her arms over her chest. "Maybe that's true for his column in the *Chronicle*, but that doesn't mean we can't land a good rating on his blog. I'd like to earn five utensil rolls from him. It feels like a second chance."

Jacob reared back from the grill. "He has a blog? And he's ripping off the Gourmet Guy's utensil roll rating system?"

She returned to the door in time to see Raquel set the dessert plate in front of Marshall, whose face really did light up like a child's on Christmas morning. "He's not ripping off the Gourmet Guy's rating system. Marshall Fredericks *is* the Gourmet Guy."

Jacob snorted. "What are the odds of that?"

She watched Marshall take a bite of ice-cream topped pie, close his eyes briefly, and then give Raquel two thumbs-up. "It's true. Ask your brother."

A clang of a pan made her glance back to find Jacob gaping at her. "*Zane* knows Marshall Fredericks is the Gourmet Guy?"

"He just found out." She checked table four again, nodding with approval to see that Raquel had moved on to another table. "From one of his baristas."

"And he didn't tell me?"

"I take it you follow his blog too?" she asked, moving to a countertop to make sure enough vegetables and garnishes were prepped to see Jacob through the next hour or so.

"I read it every day."

"So then you know a good review on *The Gourmet Guy* would be a pretty big deal for the Hot Spot," she said, noticing that the container of green onions was low. "I'm guessing the blog has a far wider readership than our local newspaper does."

"I suppose."

After washing up, she diced a bunch of green onions and topped off the container, relishing the simple task. "So it was worth breaking protocol with a second scoop of ice cream, don't you think?"

"Without a doubt. You were right, boss."

"You'll do well to remember it," she teased, gauging that the prep work would be good for a while. She went back to the window to find the critic's plate nearly empty, his book open, and his gaze scanning the restaurant.

Hannah saw Liam step through the front door and approach the hostess stand. Seconds later, Elaine made eye contact with her through the kitchen window and beckoned.

Hannah bid farewell to Jacob and hurried through the dining room. "What's going on?" she asked.

"The chief needs a minute of your time," Elaine said, consulting her seating chart. "Table seven is open at the moment."

Hannah rested her hand on the stack of menus and smiled up at Liam. "Are you staying for dinner?"

"I wish I could, but I'm taking Gramps to a movie this evening, and I've got to get home and cleaned up before I head out to Cave City."

"Sounds fun. Tell him I said hi."

Liam nodded. "Will do. That'll make his day."

"What can I help you with?" Hannah asked.

"I didn't know if you'd heard our ruling on Miriam Spencer's house fire and thought I'd share it with you if you hadn't."

She led him to the booth Elaine had recommended, grabbing a glass of water from the drink stand as they passed it. When Liam was settled on the bench, she set the water in front of him then took the seat opposite. "I heard it was accidentally started by a mirror somehow."

He paused with the glass just shy of his mouth. "So you did hear then."

"I heard that, but I'd like to hear more if you can share," she said. "A mirror seems like such an odd way for a fire to start. Especially since most people have multiple mirrors in their homes."

"It's certainly unusual, but it's not unheard of." Liam's tone was hard to read. "First of all, the kind of mirror matters. A convex mirror will focus light differently than a concave one. A flat mirror, like you would find on a bathroom wall, will reflect light energy as well, but it's not as focused as a concave mirror."

"In Miriam's case, a makeup mirror?" Hannah asked.

Liam nodded. "Exactly. And focusing sunlight onto something like a sheet of paper or, in Miriam's case, a sheer curtain, can potentially lead to ignition."

"Wow," she murmured. "I hear what you're saying, but it still seems really improbable."

Again, Liam nodded. "I agree. On the day of the fire, there was full sun during the time frame in which it would've been streaming in that window. With the way the mirror happened to be turned, the reflected rays were concentrated on the object of combustion."

"The sheer curtains, which were probably thinner and more flammable than when they'd been hung however many years before." Hannah lowered her hands to the table and sat back. "Is that why it was hard to determine the cause of the fire? Because it actually started across the room from the heat source?"

"Yes."

"You said you ruled the fire as accidental," Hannah said. "So that means you don't think someone angled the mirror on purpose to start it?"

"I don't."

"Then I'll say it again: *wow*. But at least you figured it out, and now Miriam can claim the insurance money that she rightfully deserves."

"We're all glad it wasn't arson," Liam said.

"Anything on the brooch?" she asked. "As in how it came to be there?"

"Unfortunately, so many people were in that house between the fire and when you discovered the brooch that the sheriff's fingerprint dusting turned up many, many sets."

"But what about on the brooch itself? I know mine would be on there, along with Miriam's, Tom's, and Lacy's. But is there another set besides?"

"I don't know. My guess is that with so many people handling it, they'd be smudged even if there were more, but I'll check with the sheriff on that and report back."

"That would be great, Liam. Thank you."

"My pleasure." He eyed her across the rim of his glass. "Any luck on finding another friend Michael Spencer might have had around the time the brooch went missing?"

Hannah shook her head. "No. Just the one you told me had died, Donald Holtmeyer. Even if he knew about it, he couldn't be our polisher any more than Michael could be."

"I'm sorry."

"No, *I'm* sorry. I didn't want Michael to have taken it because of how that might affect Miriam's memories of him, but I wanted to figure out the truth for you and your grandfather." She traced her finger along the edge of the table as she revisited her time with Miriam in her head. "I still wish I could do that."

"You found the brooch, Hannah. That's good enough," he said.

"Having that brooch go missing hurt your grandmother too, Liam. She felt horrible that something that had been part of your family for so long disappeared after it was given to her. Miss Bridget was such a huge part of my life growing up that I suppose I wanted to clear her name."

"It wasn't her fault. Clearly."

"She didn't know that when it went missing, or at any point afterward," Hannah protested.

"But now *we* know it, thanks to you."

She leaned forward as a thought struck her. "Hey, is there any chance your grandfather might know who lived in Miriam's house right before she and her husband moved into it in the fall of 1966?"

"I can ask him. But why does it matter?"

"Because maybe *that's* the person who stole the brooch. That would explain why Miriam didn't know anything about it."

He finished his water and set the empty glass off to one side. "That certainly sounds like a fair guess. I'll talk to Gramps and give you a call tonight if it's not too late. How long do you tend to be awake?"

"I don't get upstairs to my apartment until close to eleven most nights, and then I need a good forty-five minutes to an hour to unwind. So I'm usually up until midnight or so."

"Perfect." He slid to the end of the bench and stood. "If it's later than that, I'll give you a call in the morning. Have a great night, Hannah."

"You too, Liam." She watched him make his way to the door, hold it open for a young woman, and then disappear onto the street as the door swung closed in his wake.

For a moment, she remained where she was, soaking in the expressions of her customers, their smiles, laughs, and relaxed demeanors. It was everything she'd wanted when she'd dreamed about opening her own restaurant one day. And now here it was, right in front of her eyes.

Any worry she'd had that the people of Blackberry Valley might not embrace the new restaurant was dissipating. The Hot Spot was busy every night, and she was beginning to recognize repeat customers. Even the review in the *Blackberry Valley Chronicle*—

She swung her focus over to the table where the critic had sat as her thoughts continued on to the pictures and paraphernalia she wished had been up on the walls before Marshall Fredericks had returned. Then again, if his smile as he'd interacted with Raquel was any indication, he'd be back. And when he was, the firehouse theme he'd thought too light would be everywhere, thanks to Liam and Patrick Berthold, as well as Hannah's father.

"Boss? Is everything okay?'

Hannah smiled up at her waitress. "Hey, Raquel. Yes, I'm fine. Just woolgathering." She rose from the table and stretched. "I notice the reviewer has left."

"He has. Unfortunately."

Hannah didn't miss the disappointment in Raquel's tone. "I take it that means he wasn't difficult to wait on."

Raquel ducked her head, her cheeks darkening with a blush. "He was great, actually. Polite. Appreciative. Complimentary. And a fellow ice cream fan."

"He *did* seem quite pleased with his dessert." Hannah grinned.

Raquel laughed and nudged her shoulder. "He was quite pleased with everything he ate. Which has to be good, right?"

"It certainly could be," said Hannah. "If we're lucky."

Raquel patted her apron pocket. "He tipped really well too."

"I'm glad. I know you deserve every cent and then some." Hannah glanced toward the front of the restaurant, where the woman Liam had encountered on his way out chatted with Dylan while Elaine retrieved a menu. "Do you know who that is?"

"I don't. But it looks like Elaine is getting ready to put her in my section, so I better go."

"Thanks, Raquel." She followed her to the hostess stand and Dylan as Raquel broke off and followed Elaine with their latest customer. "Hey, Dylan. All good so far?"

Dylan set a customer's bill beside the register and ran the payment. "It's been pretty much nonstop all night."

"That's a Friday night for you. People don't want to cook after a long week of work."

The small printer beside the register spat out a receipt, and Dylan tore it off. "Remember the other day when someone was asking you about Penelope McIntosh? That's her." He nodded to the table where Raquel stood, pointing out several items on the menu to the young woman, who had perched her sunglasses on top of a crop of unruly dark blond hair.

"Penelope told me she got a job out at your friend's farm. I think she likes it so far. I have to get this receipt to my customer," Dylan said.

"Don't forget to tell them about the comment form on our website." At the end of the month, Hannah would randomly select a winner from those who had filled out the form. The prize was a free dinner for two at the Hot Spot.

"I've been telling everyone," he assured her.

"Thanks, Dylan."

She chatted briefly with Elaine about the steady turnover of tables and then went to greet Lacy's new employee. "Welcome to the Hot Spot. You're Penelope, right?"

The young woman raised her head. "I am. Have we met?"

"No. I'm Hannah Prentiss. My best friend, Lacy Minyard, is—"

Penelope set down her glass of soda. "Lacy Minyard? I just started working for her out at her farm."

Hannah smiled. "I didn't come over to interrupt your night. I just want to introduce myself and welcome you to my restaurant."

Penelope's throat moved with a hard swallow as her pale blue eyes moved to take in their surroundings. "This is your restaurant?"

"It is."

"I know Dylan." Penelope wrapped her hand around her glass. "Or rather, I *sort of* know him. We met at the coffee place when I was looking for a job. He told me he'd gotten the job I'd been told about here, so I kept looking around."

Hannah nodded. "He mentioned that to me. And I know you found a good situation with Miriam Spencer, at least for a little while."

"H-how do you know about that?" Penelope stammered. Was it Hannah's imagination, or had she turned a little pale?

"Because I'm friends with Miriam," Hannah said. "She said you were a real blessing to her in the short time you worked for her."

Penelope coughed as if to clear her throat and then took a long drink of her soda. When she finished, she slowly lowered the glass back to the table. "Working there was surreal."

"How so?" Hannah asked.

"I got a glimpse of the past while I was there." Penelope opened her utensil roll and carefully arranged the silverware on top of her napkin. "Which was cool, you know? And she was really nice. She gave me a gift card when she told me that she had to let me go sooner than she'd promised."

Hannah recalled her last conversation with Miriam and the joy her friend had clearly gotten from Penelope's willing ears. "Miriam is a special and interesting person, no doubt. I'm sorry she had to deal with a fire, and sorry you had to hunt for a job again. Though Lacy is fantastic, and I know she appreciates the extra pair of hands. We get our eggs and some of our vegetables from Bluegrass Hollow Farm, and it's because the product is good, not because Lacy and I have been friends forever."

"I love the animals," Penelope said.

Hannah smiled. "I do too. Don't tell her, but I almost wish I could have one of Mimi's kids once they're finally born."

"Do you think she might let you have one, since you've been friends for so long?" Penelope asked.

"Oh, she definitely would. And I'd take her up on it if I didn't live in a one-bedroom apartment upstairs." Hannah chuckled. "But I do, so I'll just have to settle for being a goat auntie, I guess."

Penelope's answering laugh was quickly followed by a sigh of delight as Raquel reappeared at the table with a basket of fresh bread and a bowl of farm-fresh butter. "That smells heavenly. Really."

"I'm glad. I'll let you enjoy it in peace." Hannah started to back away, but Penelope held out a hand.

"Please stay, if you can. I'm enjoying our conversation. Do you like living above your business?" Penelope selected a slice of bread.

"I do. Especially while I'm getting the Hot Spot off the ground."

Penelope spread a layer of butter over the bread then used it to indicate the crowded tables around them. "Looks to me like it's off the ground."

Hannah took in the bustling dining room and the constant movement of her waitstaff. "We're getting there, slowly but surely."

"It seems to be a welcome addition in this town."

"For which I am very grateful," Hannah said. "So where did you move here from?"

"Tennessee."

"The mountains there are gorgeous. Did you come from one of those regions?"

The young woman took another bite of bread. "Sort of."

"I see. Do you have friends or family who live here in town?"

Penelope swallowed hard then cleared her throat. "No."

"Then what made you pick Blackberry Valley, Kentucky, of all places?" Hannah asked.

"I closed my eyes and pointed at a map, believe it or not." Penelope grabbed her soda glass again. "What about you? I'm guessing that if you've been friends with Lacy for so long, you must've grown up in this town just like she did."

"I did. But I left for college and stayed away for a decade."

"Why did you stay away, and what brought you back?" Penelope asked.

"I stayed in California for school and then to build my experience. I came home because I finally realized I was spending all my time and effort helping my bosses achieve *their* dreams rather than trying to achieve my own. So I came back to try my hand at it myself."

"I totally get that," Penelope enthused. "If we don't go after what we want or what should've been ours all along, who will, right?"

Raquel appeared beside the table again, this time with Penelope's dinner—the Pull Box sandwich with a side of macaroni and cheese. "Dinner is served." Raquel set the plate and a small cup of barbecue sauce in front of Penelope and then reached into her apron pocket for two packages of hand wipes. "Is there anything else I can get you? More bread or soda?"

"No, everything's great," Penelope said. "Thank you."

"I'm going to leave you to enjoy your meal now, Penelope, but it was really great chatting with you," Hannah told her as Raquel hurried away. "Best wishes with the new job. I hope Blackberry Valley proves to be everything you want it to be and more."

"So do I, Hannah. So do I."

Chapter Sixteen

Yawning, Hannah carried her spoon and bowl of cereal to the couch and sank down into her favorite corner. A banana, some sliced strawberries, and the second cup of coffee she'd brought in earlier waited on the coffee table she'd found at a yard sale.

She switched on the TV. The same two news anchors who greeted her every Saturday morning appeared in response, alert and energetic without a single hair out of place.

"Good morning," said the male anchor. "We may be starting this Saturday on a relatively quiet note across the viewing area, but that was most definitely not the case over in Cave City, where flames from a five-alarm fire in a vacant building could be seen for miles, requiring the assistance of firefighters from several neighboring municipalities, including Blackberry Valley."

Hannah froze with her spoon halfway to her mouth.

"Let's go out to Cave City with our field reporter, Ginger Sweeney, who is standing by near the site of what became a grueling night for nearly two dozen firefighters. Ginger, what can you tell us?"

Hannah watched as the face of the blond, thirtysomething news anchor was replaced by that of a wide-eyed twentysomething standing in front of what remained of a smoldering pile of rubble.

"Good morning, Reece," Ginger said. "It was, indeed, an arduous night on Minor Avenue in Cave City. The initial call reporting the blaze came to the Cave City Fire Department shortly after eleven o'clock last night. Less than five minutes later, when the first truck arrived on scene, the flames had already reached the top of the three-story building and were threatening to consume the structures on either side. That's when officials put out the call for backup from far and wide, and our neighbors certainly delivered. Let's take a look at action during the thick of the fire."

Hannah dug in for another spoonful of cereal but stopped as the view changed to one of a dark night sky awash in orange flames. She could see firefighters of all shapes and sizes decked out in their gear, spraying water, hustling around, and calling to one another as the fire raged behind them.

As she watched, the camera panned left, giving her a brief view of—

The chirp of her phone alerted her to an incoming text, and she set her bowl and spoon down. She picked up the device and felt the rest of her morning fog dissipate at the sight of the name on her screen—Liam Berthold.

HEY, HANNAH. I'M SORRY I DIDN'T REACH OUT LAST NIGHT. A CALL CAME IN AFTER I DROPPED GRAMPS OFF THAT TOOK OVER THE REST OF MY NIGHT. I DID ASK HIM WHO OWNED MIRIAM'S HOUSE BEFORE SHE DID. HE SAID IT WAS A FAMILY FROM OUTSIDE BV WHO DIDN'T STAY LONG. MAYBE A YEAR OR TWO. DOESN'T RECALL NAMES. GRAMPS HAD A GOOD IDEA THOUGH. NEIL AT LEGEND & KEY BOOKSTORE IS A WEALTH OF INFO ABOUT EVERYTHING. MAYBE HE CAN HELP YOU. HEADING TO BED NOW. GOOD LUCK.

She'd assumed that his lack of reaching out had been work-related, but having him take the time to apologize and explain when he owed her neither was…nice. Thoughtful. Refreshing.

Quickly, she typed a reply. NEIL IS A GOOD IDEA. THANKS. GLAD YOU'RE SAFE. SLEEP WELL. YOU EARNED IT.

She returned to the couch and finished her breakfast, going through her plans for the morning—plans that now included a stop at Legend & Key Bookstore.

She stepped beneath the bell that alerted Lacy's husband, Neil, to the arrival of new customers and pulled the door closed behind her, her senses immediately shifting into overdrive.

The sight of the many floor-to-ceiling bookshelves teeming with hardcover, trade, and mass-market paperbacks was more than a little overwhelming—but in a good way. No matter which way she turned, there were stories waiting to be devoured.

The distinctive aroma of paper and print and old dust jackets was akin to the smell of food cooking for the booklover she'd been since childhood.

The quiet sound of books being removed from shelves and pages being turned served as both a tantalizing tease and a silent commitment to herself to make time to read for at least a little while during her upcoming two days off from the restaurant. Yes, she had invoices to pay, orders to place, marketing to plan, and memorabilia to frame and hang, but somewhere, amid all of that, she would find time to read. She needed it, and she knew from experience that nothing would burn her out faster than not taking time for herself.

Aware of a growing restlessness in her hands, she stepped to the nearest shelf, her fingers longing to reveal the title and cover of the baby-blue spine that called to her like—

"Hello, Hannah. To what do I owe the pleasure of having you in my shop this morning?"

She smiled at Neil as he stepped out from behind the counter. "Hi, Neil." She gestured to the shelf she'd been inches away from touching. "I have to ask, does the invisible magnet you put inside your cozy mysteries attract everyone as strongly as it does me, or am I just that weak?"

"If being pulled toward books is a sign of weakness, Hannah, I am in serious, *serious* trouble, I'm afraid," Neil replied, indicating the walls of books all around them.

She laughed. "You have one of the coolest jobs ever. After mine and your wife's, anyway."

"You haven't mucked stalls all that often, have you?" Neil quipped.

"Okay, so maybe the mucking part doesn't qualify as 'cool,' but growing amazing fruits and vegetables, gathering your own eggs, and tending to adorable animals are all pretty cool activities in my book."

"In mine, as well. Though, truth be told, the very top spot on my personal list of cool things—above homegrown food, books, and even baby goats—belongs to Lacy."

"I couldn't agree more," Hannah said. "Opening my restaurant has been amazing, but being back here with my dad, my uncle, and Lacy is everything I wanted for so long."

"Blackberry Valley is glad to have you, and not just because you've brought us a great new restaurant." Neil stepped behind the counter and took up his station at the computer. "So, is there something in particular you're after, or are you here to browse?"

"I'm actually here to pick your brain about something, if that's okay."

He leaned against the counter. "Of course. What can I help you with?"

"Your love of maps." She pointed at the partition above his head and the walls on either side of the counter. "Specifically, your expertise in reading antique maps. I know from conversations we've had over the years that one of the things you find most fascinating about older maps is the story they tell and how they speak to people's views of the world at the time the map was made. But I also know they can show you how geography has changed over time. I know you're most focused on maps of other countries, but have you spent any time with old local maps?"

"I assume that by 'local' you mean Blackberry Valley," he replied. "Yes, I've spent some time with some old maps of the area. Biggest change from the earliest ones to now is all the new roads and houses."

"Do they ever tell you who lived in a particular house during a certain time?" she asked.

"Not that I've seen. It's more about boundary lines and roads."

She sighed. "Oh. Okay. It was kind of a long shot anyway, I suppose. I didn't really think they would, but I was hoping I just didn't know old maps."

Neil tilted his head. "Why do you ask?"

"I was wondering about past residents."

"In Blackberry Valley at large?" Neil asked. "Or on a specific street?"

"More like a specific house."

"Oh, I can help you there. You can get that a couple of ways."

"Really? How?"

"You can check with the tax assessor. Depending on how long and how well they've kept property tax records, they should be able to provide a list of every owner of a given property."

"I'll try that," she said. "What's the other way?"

"The county clerk," Neil replied. "They have records of deed owners, past and present, that'll include not only names, but also dates."

Her gaze snapped to his. "The county clerk can tell me who and when?"

"They should be able to, yes."

"Can I simply show up and ask, even if it's about a property I don't own and never have?" she asked.

"I think you can, but I know for sure you can research whatever you want at the library."

She stared at him. "The library?"

"The local history section, to be exact. If you haven't checked it out, you should. It's fascinating."

"Actually, I was there yesterday morning. Did you know they have all the yearbooks from Blackberry Valley High School?" She set her bag on the counter and reached inside for a notebook and pen. "Are there town record books about houses or something?"

"I know they have archived maps, and I'm pretty sure I've seen original building plans for some structures. Between that and old photographs, as well as newspaper articles that might identify where people lived, you should be good." He tapped her notebook. "And don't forget the Sunshine Club records."

"What is that, and what would those show me?" Hannah asked, writing as fast as she could.

"The Sunshine Club connects local high schoolers with lonely shut-ins. It's a way for the high schoolers to build community service hours for scholarship applications, though I think they get a lot more out of it than that. In fact, most graduates stay in touch with people they connected with through the Sunshine Club."

"I remember that club now, but what does it have to do with what I need?" Hannah asked. "I wasn't involved with it in high school."

"To find people who might like their services, the club used to canvass people at their homes and take residential information," Neil told her. "I believe they based their questionnaire on census records to make sure it was thorough. That practice stopped in the '90s when concerns arose about privacy, but if I'm not mistaken, the library kept the records the club collected before that. If you're after details about a specific property during the time they did the canvassing, the Sunshine Club records can tell you how many people lived there and their occupations. What time frame are you interested in?"

"I'd like to learn who lived in Miriam Spencer's house right before she and her husband, Michael, moved into it in the fall of 1966."

Neil chuckled. "I wish I could answer that for you off the top of my head, but that predates me by quite a few years, making me rather useless, I'm afraid."

"You've been anything but useless," Hannah said, reviewing her notes. "You've given me things to try I never would have thought of myself. Thank you."

"I'm glad to help."

She checked the time. "Actually, I might be able to squeeze in some time at the library before I need to get to the restaurant."

His phone rang. He glanced at the screen then held up a finger. "It's Lacy. Hang back for a second, okay? That way I don't get in trouble for not putting you on to say hi."

"As if that would happen," Hannah said.

"You're her best friend."

"And you're her husband and the love of her life."

He grinned. "Which makes me one very lucky guy, doesn't it?" He picked up the phone and held it to his ear. "Hello, my love. Guess who's standing here with me right now?"

She waited for Lacy to say *who* and Neil to reply with her name. Instead, she watched Neil's eyes widen as he stood transfixed by words she couldn't hear.

"Is everything okay?" she whispered.

He held up a finger in a silent request for her to wait. "I'll tell her," he said into the phone. "And of course I want pictures—lots and lots of pictures. Good luck. I'll say some prayers. Call me when you can. I love you too."

She leaned across the counter as he put the phone away. "What's going on? *Prayers?* Is everything okay?"

Neil beamed at her. "Definitely. Mimi is about to have her kids."

"Right now?"

"It certainly sounds that way."

She clapped her hands with excitement. "Do you want me to cover for you here so you can go?"

He waved a hand at her. "I'm a books-and-maps guy, not a veterinarian."

"Oh, come on, Neil. You love your animals. I've caught you chatting about maps with Razzle Dazzle and your favorite books with Hennifer."

"That's true. But Lacy is better with this kind of stuff. I'd probably be in the way more than anything else, and I really should be here. Saturdays can be busy for me, since fewer people are at work."

She grabbed her tote bag off the counter. "Then *I'm* going. If nothing else, I'll make sure to get pictures for you."

He walked her to the door, amusement playing across his clean-shaven face. "Didn't you want to know who lived in Miriam Spencer's house before she did?"

"I did, but that can wait. I want to be there when Mimi has those babies."

"*Kids*," Neil corrected, grinning.

The bell jingled above her head as she pulled the door open and stepped out into the late morning sun. "Call them whatever you want. All I know is I can't wait to hold them."

Chapter Seventeen

"That was amazing," Hannah whispered as she took in the three kids on wobbly legs nursing for the very first time. One was a warm cinnamon brown, one black, and the third white. Mimi stood completely still, occasionally making murmuring sounds that Lacy had called mumbling. It was a soothing noise that reassured her kids. "And look at Mimi. It's as if she's done this a million times."

Crouching nearby, Lacy nodded. "She's doing so well, especially considering first-time mama goats usually have only one or two, and here she is with three. A living, breathing reminder of God's awesomeness, isn't it?"

"Without a doubt." Hannah admired the little goat family. "For the record, if I didn't live in a small apartment above the restaurant, I'd so want one. But only with your permission, Mimi."

"I'm sure she'd agree. Can you take another picture of them for me?" Lacy asked. "And maybe get me in this one too? Neil would like that."

Hannah carefully aimed her friend's phone and snapped the photo. "I definitely got you in some of the pictures along the way too, but this one is priceless."

Lacy grinned. "Baby goats have that effect."

Hannah snapped a few more shots then took a selfie with the group.

"Penelope? Would you like Hannah to get one of you with them, as well?" Lacy asked.

The young woman raised her head from where she was cleaning up the various towels and implements used during the birth. Her face lit up. "I would love that. Yes, please!" She patted her pockets and groaned. "I think I left my phone next to my bag at the front of the barn."

Hannah held up her phone. "No problem. If you want to give me your number, I could take the photos and send them to you. Or I'd be happy to get your phone and take some with that."

"Could you get mine?" Penelope asked. "I'd really appreciate it, and that'll give me time to wash my hands and make myself a little more presentable."

"Of course." Hannah glanced back at Lacy. "Are you good for a moment?"

"We're good."

Hannah smiled again at the precious new life and then made her way out of the stall toward the early-afternoon sun streaming in through the barn's expansive front doors. When she reached them, she glanced around for Penelope's bag. To her right were the rakes used for mucking, and to her left was a shelf of neatly folded horse blankets. Below that was a large, beige, drawstring bag, tipped over with some of its contents spilled onto the floor alongside a phone.

"That's strange." She scanned the area for potential culprits and spotted Rocky the rooster peering around the door at her. "Rocky? Did you knock Penelope's bag over?"

Rocky disappeared back outside.

"An admission of guilt if I've ever seen one." Hannah righted the bag, gathered the package of tissues and wrapped candies that had scattered from the opening, and—

She paused as her gaze fell on the photograph inside Penelope's bag. The image was a bit out of focus and lacked good light but somehow struck a familiar chord.

The brown-and-white afghan folded on the foot of a full-size bed. The high-backed chair. The old-fashioned dresser with a makeup mirror, a small jewelry box, a framed picture, and a silver hairbrush, comb, and hand mirror on top.

The room's sheer white window curtain was reflected in the oval makeup mirror.

Hannah pulled the photo from the bag. "Why is Penelope carrying around a picture of Miriam Spencer's guest room?"

Her confusion growing, she peeked into the bag and found a black-and-white image. From the angle the shot was taken, she couldn't see the eastern redbud trees on the left side. The pair of rockers she and Miriam had sat on weren't on the porch, but even without them she recognized the place. What she didn't understand was why Penelope had a picture of Miriam's house.

Then again, before coming to work for Lacy at the farm, Penelope had worked for Miriam—cleaning, weeding, running errands, and being an occasional lunch companion for the elderly woman. In fact, there was a photo of Miriam in the bag. Hannah's friend smiled up at her, her emerald-green eyes a near-perfect match to her housecoat. She was clearly in the middle of one of her animated stories, her hands in midair. She seemed to Hannah to be as regal as any queen holding court, even from a rocking chair on a porch in Kentucky.

Miriam had shared her appreciation for Penelope's work ethic and presence with Hannah. And now, thanks to the photos, Hannah realized that the time spent with Miriam had meant something to Penelope, as well.

Smiling, she carefully slid the photos into the bag and closed it. She straightened and hurried back to the stall where Lacy and Penelope were cooing over the new kids.

"I've got your phone," Hannah announced. "Ready for your picture?"

Penelope's smile spread fast and wide. "Absolutely!"

Hannah stepped into position, tapped the camera icon, and framed the perfect shot of Lacy's new helper alongside the farm's newest tenants. She took a few shots and then held up the phone. "Do you want this with you, or do you want me to put it back in your bag?"

"I'll take it." Smiling, Penelope reached for the phone, swiped through the photos Hannah had taken, and then slid it into her pocket. "Thanks, Hannah."

"Have you ever helped with a goat birth before?" Hannah asked her.

Penelope laughed. "No. Never. I've worked a lot of different jobs in a lot of different places over the past few years, but this is my first time working on a farm."

"Do you like it?"

"Yes," Lacy said for her. "She likes it very, *very* much—so much, in fact, that she'll stay on and work here forever. Right, Penelope?"

The three women laughed, and Hannah nudged Lacy. "Sounds like you've found the right fit for a job that Neil and I have been after you to fill for ages."

Lacy lifted her hands, palms out. "Okay, okay. You're right. Yes, having Penelope here the past two days has been great. Yes, I should've done it sooner. But if I had, Penelope wouldn't have been available."

"Because you were working for Miriam Spencer, right?" Hannah asked Penelope.

Penelope shifted her weight and crossed to the bucket of towels she'd abandoned in favor of getting a picture. "Yes. But like I told you at the restaurant, because of the fire, her visit with her son went on longer than expected. When she was able to come back, he decided to stay on with her. Which I imagine she's enjoying since he is…family."

Hannah noted the young woman's change in pitch when referencing Tom. "I take it you met Tom?"

"I did." Penelope's jaw tightened.

"Was there some kind of issue?"

Penelope shook her head. "Not on my end. I got the impression he wasn't thrilled she hired me."

Hannah was even more puzzled—and intrigued. How could Tom have a problem with someone being on hand to help his aging mother? "You specifically?"

"I don't think so. I heard him say something to her before I even met him about how she should have checked with him first."

"What do you think the issue was?" Hannah asked.

Penelope appraised Hannah as if trying to figure out whether to trust her. Finally, she said, "I think his problem was that Mrs. Spencer was paying me."

Hannah nodded, understanding at last. She'd heard of adult children who took issue with their parents spending money in ways they thought unnecessary. "Miriam is a competent woman, capable of making her own decisions. And for what it's worth, I know she loved having you around and that she misses you very much."

"You mentioned her last night," Penelope said. "I'm guessing that means you two are close?"

"I'd like to think so. I've known Miriam since I was a little girl."

"Oh, that's right, you grew up in Blackberry Valley." Penelope scooped up one last towel, added it to her bucket, and looked at Lacy then Hannah. "And you're both—what? Midthirties?"

"We're both thirty-five," Hannah said.

Lacy held up a hand. "Yes, but I'm younger by about six months."

Hannah rolled her eyes. "As I recall, you couldn't stand that when we were in grade school."

Penelope picked up the bucket. "How long has your family been in this area, Lacy?" she asked.

Lacy sat on the ground again and held out her finger for the cinnamon-colored kid to smell while modulating her voice so as not to scare it away. "Several generations. This farm has actually passed down through my family for years and years, and when my dad died, my mom passed it to me."

Penelope cleared her throat. "I imagine your grandparents must be super proud of the way you take care of this place, huh?"

"They're gone now." Lacy held her fingers steady as the second of the three kids wobbled over to her for a curious sniff. "But I'd like to think they would be."

"They would be, Lacy," Hannah said. "I'm certain of that."

"So you probably grew up hearing all sorts of old stories about Blackberry Valley and its residents," Penelope said. "That must have been fascinating."

"Probably, but unfortunately I don't remember many details." Lacy fell silent as the final kid joined its siblings while their mother looked on.

Hannah carefully picked up her phone and aimed the camera at her best friend. "This is it," she said. "The most perfect shot of the day."

"Will you send it to Neil for me?" Lacy asked as Hannah lowered the phone.

"Already on it." Hannah attached the photo to a text and sent it. "He'll love that one."

"Thanks, Hannah."

"No, thank *you*."

Lacy gave her a startled expression. "For what?"

"For letting me be here, gawking through Mimi's birth experience, so I could welcome these little ones into the world with you. Which reminds me—they need names."

"You're right, they do." Lacy scratched the black kid's chin. "I think this one should be Flower." She patted the white one's head. "And this one is Niblet."

"How sweet," Hannah said. "Welcome to the world, Flower and Niblet."

Lacy tapped the nose of the cinnamon-colored one. "And this one has no name. Yet."

"So what are you waiting for?" Hannah asked. "She needs one."

"You're right, she does." Lacy lifted her gaze to Hannah's. "So, get to work. I want an answer by the time I see you at church tomorrow."

Hannah drew back. "You want *me* to name her?"

"You've been calling the role of auntie for the past month or so, haven't you?"

"Yes. But that doesn't mean you have to let me name her. It just means I want to be their special person—the one who gets to show up and spoil them all without having to do any of the hard stuff."

"You will be," Lacy said. "So you'd better make that name a good one."

Hannah threw her arms around her friend, earning startled glances from all three kids along with a bleat of irritation from Mimi for the interruption. "Sorry, Mama. And don't worry. I'll come up with the perfect name for your sweet little one."

"I can't wait to hear it," Lacy told her.

Glancing down at her watch, Hannah reluctantly made herself back away. "Duty calls. But thank you so much, Lacy. This was amazing, and I hope to be able to do it more often in the future."

"Me too," Lacy agreed. "Kids, say goodbye to Auntie Hannah."

The goats bleated as if they understood, and Hannah chuckled as she reached the gate. "Penelope? It was nice experiencing this with you today, and I'm glad we got a chance to know each other a little better."

Penelope was washing out towels in the barn's industrial sink. "You too, Hannah. Thanks."

"One of these days maybe I can bring Miriam here with me so you can visit with each other a little," Hannah suggested.

If the young woman heard her over the water, she gave no indication. Hannah debated doubling back to a spot where she could be more easily heard, but another peek at her watch nixed that idea. She ran for her car.

There'd be time to talk to Penelope some other time.

Chapter Eighteen

It was, without a doubt, the Hot Spot's best Saturday yet, with customers sticking around for up to half an hour to get a table at the height of the dinner rush.

As usual, Raquel took it all in stride. She hustled from table to table, taking orders, filling drinks, delivering meals, processing payments, and still engaging customers with the kind of chitchat that left smiles in her wake.

Dylan hustled too, but his interaction with his customers went no further than politely taking orders and making sure they were happy with their food. It was the reason Raquel's tips were always higher than Dylan's. But he was a work in progress—one who'd already made huge strides in just the past month. He would learn to build rapport with his customers.

"You look like my mom right now," Raquel said, stepping up beside Hannah. "Smiling because someone did something that made her proud."

Hannah grabbed a cloth from the bussing container and began wiping down a four-top. "Well, Dylan's come a long way since he started. He hasn't dropped a tray, spilled anything, or forgotten to collect a payment this entire week, *and* he's been keeping up unbelievably well tonight."

Raquel sniffled and pretended to wipe away a tear. "Our baby is growing up."

"He sure is," Hannah said, laughing as she returned to her own task. "If he's a little dejected at the end of the night because he did everything right and still got less in tips than you, encourage him to add in a little pizzazz. Like you do."

Raquel wiggled her shoulders. "You think I have pizzazz?"

Hannah rolled her eyes. "Yes, I do." She saw another group come in the door. "You're up."

Raquel gave her a mock salute and hurried away.

Hannah crossed back to the bussing container, dropped the cloth inside, and gave Elaine a thumbs-up at the hostess stand.

Elaine led a group of four men toward the table—one in jeans and a sky-blue Henley, another in black cargo shorts and a white T-shirt, the third sporting jeans and a golf shirt, and the last one wearing a traditional pair of tan khakis and—

"Fancy meeting you here," Liam said as he passed the chair his friends had left open for him and came to meet Hannah instead. He motioned around the dining room. "We tried to get in at six, but there was a twenty-minute wait. Guys who spend the bulk of their workday waiting for something to happen aren't all that good at it when they're off. So we walked around, befriended a stray cat in the park, stopped at the market and bought a can of food for said stray cat, watched the rookie climb a tree none of us believed he could actually climb, and then made our way back in the hope we could get a table without waiting. And here we are."

She took in the three seated men as they pored over their menus and then returned her attention to the town's fire chief, who cleaned up well. His black hair was neatly styled, a slight tan peeked out from the open collar of his cream-colored button-down shirt, and his chocolate-brown eyes glistened in the glow from the light fixture above.

"I'm sorry it took so long to get in," she said. "Friday and Saturday nights tend to be a restaurant's busiest time."

He held up his hands. "No, no, I wasn't complaining about the wait. I was celebrating it. Having a wait list means people either want to give your place a shot, or they already have, like us. And, like us, they enjoyed it enough that they wanted to come back."

There was no mistaking the hopeful pride Liam's praise stirred in her heart, and she felt her cheeks warm in response. "It'll be even better once I get all those amazing things from your grandfather and you up on the walls. I plan to work on that tomorrow and Monday. After church, and between marveling sessions."

"Marveling sessions?" he echoed.

"Oh, yes." She scanned the dining room, noted everything was under control, and then grabbed her phone. She pulled up an image of Mimi with her new kids and handed the phone to Liam. "They were born earlier today, and I got to be there for the whole thing."

He peered at the image. "Oh, wow. They're really cute."

"Aren't they?" Hannah enthused. "The black one's name is Flower, and the white one's name is Niblet."

"And what's the other one's name?"

Hannah couldn't stop a proud smile. "Lacy is letting me name it."

"And?" Liam asked, raising his head. "What did you choose?"

"I haven't yet. I have until church tomorrow to come up with the perfect name for her."

"Any early contenders?" he asked.

"Maybe." She reached across his hand, scrolled to a photo that focused on the cinnamon-colored kid, and smiled all over again. "The first one I thought of was Squirt."

He laughed. "Cute."

"But then, right before we opened today, I came up with Sprout."

"Sprout," he repeated, as he enlarged the kid's face on the screen. "I like that even better. I think she looks more like a Sprout than a Squirt."

"I agree. I'm going to sleep on it and see if something even more appropriate occurs to me, but for now I think I'm leaning toward Sprout." She slowly scrolled through the pictures she'd taken, letting him admire the little goats.

When she reached the selfie she'd taken with Lacy, Mimi, and the new kids, he said, "That's a great shot."

"Thanks."

"You must have been pretty excited," Liam said.

"Of course I was excited. Don't you see those beautiful little faces in the background?"

"Oh, I see them," he said. "I see all of the beautiful faces in this photo—background *and* foreground."

Before she could process what he was saying, he handed her the phone and stepped back. "Hey, I'm sorry I wasn't able to offer you anything about the previous resident of Miriam Spencer's home."

"No worries. Really." She returned her phone to the pocket of her black slacks. "Neil Minyard gave me several ideas for how to find that information. I'll try to do that on Monday too."

"When you're not marveling at baby goats," he teased.

"Exactly. Anyway, I'll leave you to your friends so you can eat. I imagine you're ready for some downtime after last night's fire."

"It was a big one," he confirmed. "And it went long. Fortunately, it was a vacant building, with no human life in jeopardy and no real memories and keepsakes to be lost."

"That's something to be thankful for." She ushered Liam toward his chair. "Now please eat and enjoy this time with your friends."

He did. Every time Hannah checked Liam's table over the next hour, he and the others clearly relished the food and the company, from a round of appetizers they shared to the entrées they raved over, and finally to the desserts that caused an argument about who had ordered the best one. As delighted as she was to see people enjoying the food, she was just as delighted to see the smiles and laughter happening *across* her food. A young couple gazed lovingly into each other's eyes over a piece of cheesecake. At another table, four women shared stories of their adult children's latest accomplishments and their own empty-nest activities. A few tables over, parents and their teenage children were engaged in an animated conversation. Beside them, an elderly man wrapped a knit shawl around his wife's shoulders with so much tenderness that it brought a catch to Hannah's throat.

"You look really happy," said a familiar voice at her side.

She watched the elderly man take his wife's hand and slowly lead her to the exit, before smiling at the freckle-faced waiter. "I *am* happy, Dylan. It's been a really good night."

"It has," he agreed. "That couple who just left was celebrating their sixty-second wedding anniversary."

"And they chose us for their special night?" She brought her hand to her chest. "Oh, I wish you'd told me sooner so I could have congratulated them."

Dylan's cheeks reddened. "I would have, but you were busy talking to the fire chief and I didn't want to interrupt." He handed her a receipt. "But I need you to take this out of my next check."

She scanned the itemized dinner items finished with a brownie à la mode. "Why? Did something go wrong with the order?"

"Not at all. This is the order for that elderly couple. They were really fun and sweet, and they reminded me a little of my grandparents. They were so excited to be here together, and they told me I was doing a good job. When they ordered dessert, they told me all about how they shared a brownie à la mode on their very first date, and I decided I didn't want to charge them for anything. So I want you to take it out of my check."

"Not a chance." She looked him in the eyes. "You did the right thing. And you've reminded me of something I should have said to both you and Raquel when we started last month. I want each of you to have the ability to choose a table once in a while—preferably a two-seater, but we can talk about it more depending on circumstances—for which you can comp an appetizer or a dessert for a special occasion."

"But I comped them their whole tab," Dylan objected.

"That's not a problem this time. I'll take care of it."

Dylan beamed at her. "Thanks, Hannah."

"It's my pleasure. Now, I think one of your tables needs you." She tipped her chin toward a woman who was trying to get Dylan's attention.

As Dylan hurried away, Hannah glanced back at the table where the elderly couple had been sitting and caught a glimpse of something on the seat. When she reached it, she saw that it was a silver-handled brush that must have fallen out of the woman's purse. She took it up to Elaine. "That elderly couple who just left? I think the woman left this behind."

Elaine set it on the bottom shelf of the hostess stand. "The man said they were going to go for a romantic anniversary stroll, so maybe they'll walk past here on their way back to their car."

"Perfect. Thanks, Elaine. And if you do see them again, please wish them a happy anniversary from all of us here at the Hot Spot."

Three hours later, after the kitchen was clean, the dining room was freshly vacuumed, and her excellent staff had exited, Hannah locked the front door and allowed herself the satisfied sigh she'd more than earned. While she couldn't be happier with the way the night had gone, she was ready—eager, actually—to have the next two days off.

Yes, she had plans that would take up the bulk of that time, but that was okay. Especially when so many of them came with the opportunity to be around the very people who had played such a huge factor in her decision to move back to Blackberry Valley.

She rested her forehead against the glass and took in the lanterns that dotted the main road through town. As a little girl, she'd walked this same street countless times, hand-in-hand with her mother on their way to the store, the library, or the park beyond the town hall.

As vivid as those memories were, so too were the ones that included walking past the very building in which she now stood. Back then, the door had been solid wood squares rather than the pair of arched doorways she'd had custom-made to fill the garage-style opening. Now, instead of a space inhabited by a shiny red fire truck and walls lined with boots and coats, there were tables and chairs at which people sat to enjoy dishes she and her chef had fine-tuned and perfected over recent months.

She turned to take in every visible nuance of her surroundings, as she had in every restaurant she'd worked in during her time in California. But that was different now too. Rather than admiring the realization of someone else's dream, she soaked in the realization of her own. And it felt good.

So did being back in the same town as her dad and Lacy, putting down adult roots in her church, her women's group, and the community in general. She covered a jaw-cracking yawn—the first of many, she suspected.

She made one last visual inspection of her surroundings then crossed to the hostess stand and the stack of menus, which needed straightening. As she stepped back, her gaze fell on the silver brush that remained on the bottom shelf. And suddenly, she remembered seeing a different silver-handled hairbrush—bookended by a matching handheld mirror and comb.

At last, she realized what bothered her so much about the photo in Penelope's bag. Hannah could understand carrying around a picture of a friend, or even an old snapshot of a peaceful scene.

But she couldn't think of a single reason for someone to carry around a picture of a previous employer's guest room, apparently taken shortly before it had caught fire.

Chapter Nineteen

Hannah stepped out onto the front stoop of Grace Community Church and inhaled the delicate aromas of the gorgeous June morning. The exhaustion she'd felt after a night spent tossing and turning had been pushed away by Pastor Bob Dawson's sermon, and she was glad. She simply had too much to do to even consider a nap, let alone take one.

"Did you come up with a name yet?"

Turning, Hannah smiled at Lacy and Neil as they joined her. "I did."

"And?"

"Her name is Sprout."

Lacy clapped her hands in approval. "That's perfect. Mimi will be pleased."

"I hope so," Hannah said as the three of them descended the steps to the walkway below. "How were they this morning?"

Lacy exchanged a smile with her husband as he caught her hand. "Wonderful. Mimi is doing really well as a first-time mama."

"If I lived at the farm, I'd have camped out in their pen overnight so I could watch them," Hannah said.

Neil laughed. "Trust me. My wife might as well have camped out there for as many times as she checked on them during the night."

"They were barely twelve hours old," Lacy protested. "How could I not?"

"And the reason for having a babysitter for them this morning?" he teased.

Amused, Hannah met Lacy's eyes. "A babysitter?"

Lacy elbowed her husband. "I didn't feel confident leaving Mimi and the kids alone yet. If Penelope hadn't been able to sit with them, I'd have come anyway, of course. But she was, and that's given my heart peace. She's streaming a church service so she doesn't miss out."

"For me, streaming isn't the same as in-person attendance, but to each their own." Neil kissed Lacy's temple. "By the way, thanks for sending me those pictures yesterday, Auntie Hannah. It made me feel like I was there too, watching Flower, Niblet, and *Sprout* come into the world."

"It was my pleasure." Hooking her thumb beneath the strap of her purse, Hannah glanced around at the various small groups of people engaged in conversation across the church grounds, searching for the woman who'd been at the center of her troubled sleep. She spotted her talking with Connie Sanchez near the side door and politely excused herself to the Minyards.

As she neared, Miriam raised her head and made eye contact. Her easy smile disappeared, a stark reminder of their strained encounter two days ago.

"Good morning, Connie." Hannah returned the church secretary's welcoming embrace and then delivered the same to the gray-haired woman beside her. "Good morning, Miriam. You look lovely today. Greens are so beautiful on you."

Connie voiced her agreement and then left to check in with Pastor Bob. When Hannah and Miriam were alone, Hannah took the woman's hand in hers and gave it a gentle squeeze. "I'm sorry things were left on a bad note between us the other day. If I hurt you with my questions about your husband, that was not my intention. I just want to figure out how Bridget Berthold's brooch found its way under your floor."

"It wasn't Michael," Miriam said coldly, extracting her hand.

"Okay." Hannah worked to find the right way to frame one of the many questions that had plagued her during the night. "Can I ask a question about the fire? In particular, something you kept in your guest room?"

"I suppose."

Trying not to read into Miriam's tone, Hannah cleared her throat and dove in. "You once showed me a vintage dresser set you've had since you got married, and you told me that it made you feel like a princess whenever you used it."

"It did," Miriam said. "The people who lived in the house before us left it behind. When we couldn't find them to return it, Michael said I should keep it. I used it for special occasions, and I kept it displayed in the guest room the rest of the time because of how pretty it was. Losing it in the fire—along with that photo of our wedding and the afghan my mother made—hurt the most. They were just things, of course, but they were mainstays in my life for so long. It almost feels as if when they burned up, they took those pieces of my life with them."

"I'm so sorry. The most important thing, though, is that you're safe." Again, Hannah took hold of the woman's thin, hand. "I'm so thankful for that. And those pieces of your life will never be truly gone as long as they are kept safe in your heart."

This time, Miriam returned Hannah's gentle squeeze and added a small, yet genuine smile. "Thank you, dear. I believe you're right."

And with that, a little of the heaviness lifted from Hannah's mind.

"Screwdriver."

Hannah plucked the yellow-handled tool out of the metal box at her feet and offered it to her father.

"Pastor Bob's sermon this morning was really good, don't you think?" she asked as she watched her father screw one side of the firehouse bell into place.

"It certainly was. Will you hand me that other screw?" Hannah handed it up to him. "He's good at making a person reflect as well as feel God's love. Your uncle Gordon thinks so too. It's why we keep trying to get Bruce to come with us one of these Sundays."

"Bruce isn't a churchgoer?"

Dad shook his head as he tightened the final screw. "He's not. But I pray that will change—that he'll give his pain, anger, and hurt to God."

"I'll try to make a real point of talking up his design prowess in the thank-you note I'll be sending him for the display case. Because clearly his talent stretches beyond the actual act of building something. But losing an ability that was your life's work must be hard."

"It certainly doesn't help." Dad handed the tool back to Hannah and then tested the bell to make sure it was secure. When it remained in place, he climbed down the ladder to the sidewalk below. "That should do it."

"Oh, Dad, it's great!" she exclaimed. "And it still rings?"

"It should." He tugged on the chain attached to the bell, and the answering sound filled the air around them. "Success! Though we might want to tuck the chain up into the rafter when it's not in use. Otherwise, you'll have mischief-makers ringing it at all hours of the night when you're trying to sleep." He climbed the ladder once more.

"That wouldn't have mattered to me last night, but you're right. And even if I'm having a sleepless night, I'm sure my neighbors would appreciate not having their sleep interrupted." She watched him feed the chain into an opening in the rafter and then held the ladder still as he made his way back down to the ground for a thank-you hug. "This bell and all the memorabilia from the Bertholds will really hit the mark for the Hot Spot's theme. And when it's all done, I'm going to cross my fingers Marshall Fredericks returns."

"You think he will?" Dad asked.

Hannah grinned. "Based on how taken he seemed to be with Raquel, yes. He likely won't write another review so soon after the first one, but I'm hopeful he might mention us in his blog, *The Gourmet Guy*."

"I'll pray that he does." Dad closed his toolbox then searched Hannah's face, his eyes showing his concern. "Is that why you didn't sleep last night? Because you're still worried about that review?"

She smiled and patted his arm. "Actually, no. If people read the review, they don't seem to agree with his critiques. In fact, last night was our best Saturday to date." She gazed up at the bell. "And I think these extra touches will make it even better."

"Then was your lack of sleep due to adrenaline?" he asked. "From last night being such a good night?"

"No, I was plenty tired. Exhausted, even. But my mind wouldn't shut off. I kept thinking about the fire at Miriam's house—the things that survived it, and the things that didn't. And how the sun and a poorly aimed makeup mirror started it all." She stepped out of the way as her father collapsed the ladder, and then grabbed hold of one end for the walk to his truck. "I mean, that makeup mirror was on the same dresser as one that was handheld. Yet all that happened to the makeup mirror was some blackening on the glass and some soot and charring on the metal frame around it. On the other hand, the handheld mirror and its matching brush and comb melted into literally nothing."

Dad slid the ladder into the back of his truck, secured it in place with several bungee cords, and then closed the tailgate. "How do you know the one melted and the other didn't?"

"I saw the pictures from the fire's aftermath in Liam's office."

"You mean the fire chief?"

"Yes. Liam Berthold."

Dad grinned. "And what were you doing in his office? Is he someone you might be interested in dating?"

She rolled her eyes. "You've already asked this, and I've already answered it, remember? I talk to lots of people in my job, Dad. And that's all it is with Liam. My focus is on making the Hot Spot a success so I can stay here in Blackberry Valley with you, Uncle Gordon, and Lacy."

"I'm sorry. I don't mean to nag. But you'll have time and room for other things that matter in the future, right?"

She made her way around the truck to hug him again. "I don't know, Dad. Maybe one day. But today is not that day."

"Fine. I won't press," he said, opening his door. Then he winked. "For today, anyway."

"Thanks, Dad. For that, for the bell, and for understanding my need to give you a rain check on that pasta salad today. I meant to make it before work yesterday, but Mimi went into labor and threw off my plans."

"I'd be happy to stay and help hang everything up on the walls."

"I know you would, and I might ask you to do that tomorrow, if you're free. But I need to choose which items I want to use and where I want them to go before I can start hanging them."

"And don't forget those baby goats I know you're itching to see."

She smiled at the thought as he slid into place behind the steering wheel. "Oh, trust me, they're on my radar for this afternoon too."

"I'm glad to hear it, kiddo. The more things you love about being here, the less I worry that you'll change your mind and go back to California." He started the engine, pulled his door shut, and winked at her through his open window. "I love you, Hannah. You know that, right?"

"Every moment of every day." She poked her head through the opening, kissed his cheek, and stepped back. "And I love you too."

She waved as he drove away. Making her way inside, she moved toward the silver-handled hairbrush peeking out from the bottom shelf of the hostess stand. For a while, she simply stared at it, her thoughts moving between the woman who'd left it behind and the woman who'd treasured and lost a similar one.

Reaching into the back pocket of her jeans, Hannah took out her phone, scrolled through her contacts, and stopped on her most recent addition.

Liam picked up on the second ring. "Hi, Hannah."

"Hi, Liam."

"I hope you stuck with Sprout for the name," he said.

She chuckled. "I did."

"Good."

"I know it's Sunday and I shouldn't be bothering you at home, but—"

"I'm actually working."

"Fire chiefs work on Sundays?" she asked.

"When one of their guys is sick and no one else can cover, they do. Or, at least, I do. Fires don't take weekends off. But still, there's no wrong time to call."

She sank into a chair, still staring at the hairbrush. "I was hoping you could help me understand something—something I'm sure there's an explanation for, yet I'm not versed enough in fires to know."

"I'll do my best."

"If two objects were maybe a foot away from each other in a fire, why would one of them melt into oblivion while the other remained identifiable?"

"Different materials burn differently," he offered. "And perhaps the fire reached one but not the other."

"I can get that where the brush and the comb were concerned, but there's the handheld mirror that went with the set." She shook her head. "That doesn't make sense to me when the makeup mirror was largely intact."

"Wait. Is this about the fire at Miriam Spencer's? You're talking about the items on the dresser?"

"That's right. The two mirrors were pretty much next to each other. Yet her antique mirror and its matching comb and brush literally disintegrated into nothing."

In the background, she heard a sound like a drawer being opened and then pushed shut. "Okay, so I'm looking at the pictures of the guest room right now. There's no handheld mirror, brush, or comb on the dresser."

"Because the fire melted them into nothing, right?"

"Not in this fire," he said. "Not with how confined it was and how fast our response time was. It wouldn't have gotten hot enough to completely destroy something like what you're describing. The bristles of a hairbrush definitely would've melted, due to the intense heat, but the metal components would still be recognizable. And, like the makeup mirror that started the fire, the glass in a handheld mirror would be covered in soot but still identifiable as a mirror."

"Yet none of them are visible in your pictures of the dresser," Hannah mused.

"You're right, they're not. Which means they weren't on the dresser during the fire."

"But Miriam thinks they were. And I saw a photo with them on the dresser from before the fire."

"I believe you, but I'm looking at the pictures from after the fire. They're not there, so they must have been removed."

"Then I wonder where they are. Perhaps Miriam could have them back." She bit her lip, thinking. "Do you know who called in the fire?"

"Hang on." Again, she heard a drawer open and shut followed by the sound of papers being shuffled. "Here it is. The fire was called in by a young woman who worked for Miriam. She drove up outside the house, smelled smoke, and called for help."

Hannah jolted in her chair. Penelope McIntosh had called in the Spencer fire?

Chapter Twenty

Hannah pulled her Outback to a stop outside the classic red barn and cut the engine, Liam's words playing on repeat in her head as her emotions ran the gamut from confused and disbelieving to fear and even anger.

Oh, how she wanted to believe Liam's ruling on the fire was correct. That the tilt of the makeup mirror, the position of the curtains, and the strong afternoon sun had come together in an incredibly rare but perfect storm.

But try as she might on the drive to Bluegrass Hollow Farm in the wake of their call, she couldn't shake the feeling that maybe the fire wasn't an accident. That maybe something else was at play.

Or someone.

It wasn't the fact that Penelope had made the call about the fire. That made sense, since she was working for Miriam at the time. It was the antique dresser set Miriam believed had been destroyed in the fire and that Hannah had seen in a picture inside Penelope's bag.

Unfortunately, she didn't know Penelope well enough to ask her about the photos in her bag, even if she'd been able to come up with a way to explain how she'd seen them. "A rooster knocked over your bag, and I happened to see the photos when I was retrieving your phone" didn't sound plausible. No doubt Penelope would demand to know why she'd been snooping. Hannah had tried again and again to think of some sort of innocent explanation for having seen the picture, yet she came up empty each and every time.

She had so many questions. Where, exactly, had Penelope come from? Tennessee was a big place, and the young woman hadn't been particularly forthcoming about specifically where it was she'd lived there. What had brought her to Blackberry Valley? How had she ended up working for Miriam? Hannah supposed it was possible that Penelope had simply happened upon the opening during her search for work, but with the photos, it was starting to feel as if she'd targeted Miriam. Why did Penelope have a picture of the very same dresser set that was now unaccounted for?

Might the once-in-a-blue-moon fire not have been such a slim chance after all?

Hannah exited her car and made her way to the barn, stopping every few feet to greet the chickens that came to meet her. In the field to her left, she spotted Lacy's horses, Stunner, Misty, and Razzle Dazzle, nosing at the lush grass. In the meadow beyond were hundreds and hundreds of sunflowers, reaching toward their namesake in the nearly cloudless sky.

She recognized Lacy's laugh and made haste through the open barn doors, blinking rapidly as her eyes struggled to adjust to the change from direct sun to the barn's dim light. "Hello? Is anyone home?" she called, even though she knew the answer and what corner of the barn it would surely come from.

"We're back here, Hannah," Lacy called. "With Mimi and the kids."

It was hard not to smile at the knowledge that she hurried toward the trio of sweet little faces that had stolen her heart. Yet, at the same time, she was aware of a rising dread from her friend's use of the word *we*. Because while she wasn't close enough to make out the muted conversation taking place in the vicinity of her destination, she could hear enough to know that the other voice was female, and therefore not Neil's.

Drawing in a steadying breath, she came around the corner and willed her immediate smile for Lacy to stay in place for Penelope as well. She took in everything she could about her friend's new employee, searching for anything she could use to dismiss the quiet nagging in her mind. But in spite of the young woman's reciprocating smile that seemed no less genuine than Lacy's, the questions remained.

"Sprout loves her name." Lacy nodded to the cinnamon-colored kid peeking out at Hannah from behind Mimi. "Don't you, sweet girl?"

Hannah stepped inside the pen and slowly made her way closer to the barn's new additions. When she reached a distance that was close enough for them to reach her if they wanted yet not too close if they didn't, she crouched down and held out her hand. "Hi, little ones. I said a prayer for you in church today. Oh, my word, you are all so adorable. Lacy, I seriously want to take them home with me."

"I love you, Hannah, but Mimi and I aren't giving them up to be apartment goats. Are we, Mimi?"

The mother goat gave them both a disdainful eye and then stepped aside as Sprout tentatively crept toward Hannah. "Oh, she's coming over to me," she whispered. "What do I do?"

"Stay calm, hold your hand still, and don't make any quick movements," Lacy instructed. "I'll get pictures."

Hannah held absolutely still with her hand outstretched while Sprout sniffed her fingers. "She's perfect. Absolutely perfect."

"I'm sensing a little bias for the kid you named," Lacy said, chuckling.

Hannah peered past the cinnamon-colored kid at her siblings, who peeked at her from behind their mother. She gently waved the fingers of her free hand at them. "They're all adorable, every one of them."

"I'm teasing, Hannah," Lacy assured her. "I saw the way you melted when Sprout was born. That's why I let you name her. It's okay if she's your favorite."

The notion of something melting snapped her out of the euphoria of bonding with Sprout, and she stood, sending the kid skittering back to her mother and siblings. Before she could settle on her next move, though, Lacy turned to the source of Hannah's uneasiness.

"Penelope, since you came in on what was supposed to be your day off so Neil and I could go to church without worrying about the kids, why don't you come back on Tuesday morning, rather than tomorrow?" Lacy asked.

Penelope hesitated but finally said, "Uh, sure. I guess."

"Do you *want* to come in tomorrow morning?"

Penelope ducked her head, a flush creeping up her neck. "I—I could use the money. Every little bit helps, you know?"

"No problem at all. I'll always take your help. Seven o'clock tomorrow morning it is. For now, I can take it from here for the rest of the day. Thank you."

"Thank *you*." Penelope unlatched the door and slipped out of the stall. "I'll just grab my things and be on my way."

Hannah watched the young woman disappear and then faced Lacy. "I didn't see another car out there, so I didn't realize Penelope was here."

Lacy pulled a small carrot from her pocket and offered it to Mimi. "She doesn't have a car."

"Then how does she get here?" Hannah asked.

"She gets a ride from someone, or she walks."

Hannah hiked her thumb in the direction Penelope had gone. "I think I'll see if she'd like a ride to wherever it is she's living."

"You just got here," Lacy protested as Mimi accepted the carrot.

"I know, but it seems like giving Penelope a ride would be the kind thing to do."

Lacy glanced over her shoulder at Hannah. "It would be. Selfishly, though, I like having you around. You know that."

"Oh, this doesn't mean you're getting rid of me for good. I haven't gotten nearly enough baby-goat time," Hannah said, unlatching the pen door to make her exit. "I was just thinking that if I head out now to take her home, I can do all the framing and hanging of everything at the restaurant tonight, as opposed to tomorrow."

"Which means you'll be able to spend more time here tomorrow so we can really catch up?"

"Absolutely."

"Then I suppose I can allow this." Lacy's feigned sigh echoed around them. "Be kind and considerate, if you must."

Hannah's answering laugh earned her a shy glance from Sprout. "I need to be a good auntie and lead by example, right?"

Grinning, Lacy rolled her eyes. "I repeat. Go."

"I shall." Hannah waved at her friend and the sweet animals around her and then hurried to the front of the barn.

When she reached the open doorway, she glanced at the spot where Penelope's bag had been, noted its absence, and stepped outside. A glance to her right showed Lacy's horses, still grazing. On her left was the modest white farmhouse with its wide front porch and black shutters. Finally, she spotted the young woman walking along the edge of the road.

Hannah trotted to her car, hopped in, and soon caught up with Penelope. As she approached, she rolled down her window. "Hi. Can I give you a lift to wherever it is you're going?"

Penelope gave her a small smile. "It's okay. I don't have to be there until five."

Hannah checked the time on her dashboard clock. "If I take you, maybe you can fit in a little time to rest after your busy morning, and I'd love the company."

"Okay, if you're sure. Thank you."

When Penelope was settled beside her, seat belt fastened, Hannah drove on. "So, are you headed home or into town?"

"Blackberry Valley Motor Inn."

Hannah unintentionally let up on the gas pedal in her surprise. "Do you know someone who's staying there?"

"I work the evening shift there." Penelope stared out the passenger window. "In exchange for a room."

"You're living at the motor lodge?" Hannah repeated.

"I am. I have no other options," Penelope said, a hint of defensiveness edging her tone. "But it's working out. I have a roof over my head, and I'm meeting all sorts of interesting people. And goats."

Hannah mulled over the young woman's words, driving in silence for a few minutes. At the next stop sign, she turned left and headed toward the western edge of town, where both the motor lodge and Miriam's home were located.

"Do you miss working for Miriam?" she asked with a sidelong glance at her passenger.

Again, Penelope turned toward the window. "I do."

"How did you start working with her in the first place? Did she put a notice in the paper or something?"

"We crossed paths." Penelope reached down between her feet for her drawstring bag and lifted it onto her lap as the sign for the motor lodge came into view. "I needed work, and Miss Miriam needed help with some things. It just worked out. For both of us."

A block shy of the lodge, Hannah took a right.

"No, the lodge is that way," Penelope said. "This is the way to Miss Miriam's house."

"I know." Glancing at the empty road behind them in the rearview mirror, Hannah pulled to the side of the road and shifted into park. "But we need to talk. Now."

Penelope searched Hannah's face, her expression one of instant apprehension. "Talk about what?"

"The antique dresser set that was in Miriam's guest room."

The color drained from Penelope's face, and she reached for the handle of the passenger-side door.

Hannah grabbed her phone from the cupholder. "Please stay put, Penelope. If you don't, I'll have to call the police."

The tense silence stretched on as Penelope's hand remained on the door handle and Hannah gripped her phone, ready to connect a call to the sheriff's office. Eventually, though, Penelope let go of the door in favor of clutching her bag to her chest.

Hannah lowered her hand to her lap but didn't put her phone down. "You took the set, didn't you?"

Penelope swallowed hard and whispered, "Yes, I did."

Hannah's stomach sank. As much as she wanted answers for Miriam's sake, she wasn't happy with that one. It felt like a betrayal of her friend, and from someone Hannah had believed genuinely cared about Miriam. *Now to drop the other shoe.* "Did you change the angle of the makeup mirror in order to start the fire?"

Penelope's gaze shot to Hannah's, her eyes wide with horror. "No! I would never do that."

Hannah held her tongue, allowing the quiet to encourage the young woman to continue.

"Even if I could've known that would happen, I would never do anything to destroy that house," Penelope insisted. "Besides, she only had it by mistake."

Hannah held her gaze, searching for any sign the young woman was lying, but she saw only shock and revulsion at the idea of deliberately setting the fire. "Had what by mistake?"

"The dresser set—the brush, the comb, and the mirror."

"Do you mean because the previous owner left it behind?" Hannah asked. "Nearly six decades ago? They never returned to claim it, so it must not have been very important to them. But Miriam loved and cherished it."

Penelope glared through the windshield but said nothing.

"Are you so desperate for money that you chose to steal from an elderly woman rather than ask for more hours or find another job?"

Penelope's mouth tightened, yet still she remained silent.

"That set *meant* something to her, Penelope, and you let her think it burned in the fire."

Penelope's voice came out in a croak. "I'm sorry."

"When, exactly, did you take it? When you realized the room was on fire?"

"No. I took it the day after Miriam left for Cave City."

"Then why were you there when the fire started?" Hannah stopped as another thought struck. It was out there, surely, but— "Were you there to 'polish' something?"

Penelope turned to her, clearly confused. "No, Miss Miriam and I did that together the week before."

"What do you mean?"

"I did the forks and spoons, and Miss Miriam did the knives," Penelope explained. "I told her I could do them all myself, but she insisted on helping. She said it was her favorite childhood chore."

Hannah slumped in her seat. "You're talking about silverware."

"What else would I be talking about?" Penelope asked, her confusion clearly deepening.

"It doesn't matter," Hannah said. "But what's the answer to my question? Why were you there when the fire broke out?"

Penelope looked about as miserable as Hannah had ever seen anyone look. "I was going to return the dresser set," she said, her voice hardly above a whisper. "I went back a few hours later because I thought better of what I'd done. But when I got out of the car to put the set back, I smelled the fire. That's when I called 911."

Hannah stared at the girl. "What about giving it back?"

"I know I should have," Penelope said. "But with the fire and all the people there, including the police, I got scared. If I'd put it back before the fire, no one would have known it was ever missing. But if I'd put it back afterward, when the police had already taken pictures and made reports about what was damaged in the fire, someone probably would have realized that it couldn't have been there during the fire. They'd know it had been taken and then returned. The hired help is usually the first person suspected in a situation like that, right? I might never have been able to work in this area again. I wasn't thinking about that when I took it in the first place." She sniffed. "I'm really sorry."

"I'm not the one you need to apologize to—the one you need to make it right with." Hannah pointed at the bag in Penelope's lap. "Is it in there?"

Shifting in her seat, Penelope slowly loosened her hold on the bag. "It is."

"So how do you want to handle this?" Hannah asked, keeping her tone gentle. She didn't think Penelope had started the fire. "Do you want to give it to me, and I'll tell Miriam what you did?"

Penelope stared at her bag then slowly shook her head. "I want to apologize myself. I want to make it right."

"I think that's a very good call." Hannah checked her mirrors before pulling onto the street. "I'll come with you for moral support, but it's up to you whether I'm inside with you or waiting on the porch. When you're done, I'll take you to the motor lodge."

"Thank you," Penelope said, her voice breaking. "Are you going to tell Lacy?"

"No, I'm going to let you do that too. But I'll follow up to make sure you do. Lacy deserves the truth as much as Miriam."

"Do you think she'll fire me?"

"That'll be Lacy's decision to make. But if you've owned up to what you've done and you've made things right with Miriam, I think that'll go a long way for someone as caring and special as Lacy is." Hannah drove into Miriam's driveway and parked. "If she does let you stay on, you'll have to earn back her trust, as well as Miriam's and mine."

Penelope lifted her chin and met Hannah's gaze. "I know. I'll do everything I can to make that happen."

Chapter Twenty-One

Late that night, Hannah sank onto the couch in her living room, clutching Miss Bridget's journal. It was hard to believe that a mere twelve hours earlier, she'd walked out of church after Sunday service. On the one hand, it felt as if she'd been standing on her congregation's front stoop, breathing in the air's subtle floral scents, no more than a few minutes ago. But on the other hand, when she thought about everything she'd done since then, it felt like days ago.

The original firehouse bell was back in its rightful place above the front entrance.

The third of Mimi's three kids had officially been named, *and* she'd graced the tip of one of Hannah's fingers with her sweet breath and maybe even the slightest hint of a lick.

Hannah had not only figured out that Miriam's antique dresser set had been stolen, but she'd also confronted the culprit and ensured its safe return.

And nearly two dozen nods to the history of the Hot Spot's host building were now hung throughout the dining room, thanks to the many hours she'd spent framing pictures, setting up display cases, and finding the perfect place for each item.

Stretching her arms above her head, Hannah grimaced a little at the ache in her shoulders and back, but it was worth it. The memorabilia Liam and his grandfather had given her to display inside the Hot Spot had elevated its firehouse theme to a new level, proving that Marshall Fredericks had been right. All that was left to do was find a small apparatus of some kind for the area beside the front entrance. Maybe a mannequin decked out in full firefighting attire.

She lowered her hands to her lap and the journal she'd found herself thinking about far more than the latest piece of fiction she was halfway through. She thumbed past the handful of entries she'd already read and settled into her favorite corner for the next installment.

June 12, 1964

It's been a long time since I've taken time to write something in here. I've thought about it many times, but life is busy when you're engaged to be married to the man of your dreams. Every time I hear that new song by the Dixie Cups, I smile. In three short months, I'm goin' to the chapel and I'm gonna get married!

I can hardly believe it.

I've been working extra hours at the library to help pay for the wedding. I've picked out my dress, and I know I'll feel like a princess when I wear it to stand beside my prince. Mama and I have chosen the food that will be served at the reception. And Patrick has some friends who are in a band, which will add a personal touch.

I've asked Caroline to be my matron of honor, and Patrick has asked his brother, Roger, to be his best man.

Audrey will be our flower girl, and I know she will be absolutely precious in her role.

Since neither Patrick nor I have any little boys in our families, we didn't know who could be the ring bearer. And then on a picnic last week, Patrick came up with the idea of asking Jerry. Even though it had been months since I'd seen Jerry, I knew he was the perfect choice—both because of the bond we created during his mother's illness, and as something happy for him to look forward to.

But when I went in search of his father, I discovered that they've rented out their home and moved away. I'll miss my hugs from Jerry, but I pray that he and his father find their way through the pain and grief of the past year.

That means I'm back to square one on who will be our ring bearer. Perhaps one of the Prentiss boys from church would like to do it.

Hannah's mouth dropped open. "One of the *Prentiss* boys?"

She did a little math regarding Miss Bridget and Patrick's wedding and the birthdays of her father and uncle and came up with Uncle Gordon being the most likely choice at six years old, compared to her father, who would have been three at the time.

"I know what I'll be asking Dad and Uncle Gordon about the next time I see them," she said as her eyelids began to droop. Reluctantly, she closed the journal, set it on the coffee table, and yawned.

For now, it was time to call it a night.

MYSTERIES OF BLACKBERRY VALLEY

Hannah was at the Blackberry Valley Public Library the moment the doors opened at nine o'clock Monday morning, a notebook and pen lying in wait inside her tote bag. She'd been so busy with the restaurant, assisting in the arrival of Mimi's kids, and trying to figure out whether Miriam's fire was truly an accident, that her research into the previous owner of the Spencer house had been put on hold. Today, though, that was back on her agenda.

Was the mystery of who'd stolen the brooch hers to figure out? No. But Liam didn't believe the sheriff was investigating, because the brooch was back where it belonged—no harm, no foul.

Yet whoever had stolen the brooch had caused harm to Miss Bridget's heart. If Hannah could lay the case to rest, perhaps it would bring closure to her living loved ones.

At first glance, it made sense that Michael Spencer had been the brooch thief. He'd had feelings for Miss Bridget in their younger days, but she hadn't reciprocated.

Had that caused Michael to act out of a desire to sabotage her relationship with Patrick by stealing his gift to her? Perhaps he'd hoped that a rift would open up in Miss Bridget's budding relationship with Patrick as a result of her losing a precious family heirloom. It certainly seemed plausible, especially when Hannah added in the indisputable fact that the brooch had been found under a floorboard in Michael's home.

Except for one thing.

The brooch had been recently polished though Michael had passed away years before. He would have had to tell someone about the brooch before his death. But the theory of a best friend Michael might've had around the time the brooch went missing had hit a dead end.

The bothersome possibility that Michael and Miriam's son, Tom, had been behind it rattled around in her brain, but if he was as fascinated with get-rich-quick schemes as her father claimed, it was hard to imagine he wouldn't have sold it if he'd known of its existence.

She'd awakened from a sound sleep around four a.m. with the most troubling thought of all.

What if the motive she'd had for Michael to be the culprit was correct, but instead of it being *his* jealousy over Miss Bridget and Patrick's romance, it had been Miriam's? Not because Miriam had been upset the librarian and fire chief were involved, but rather because the boy *she* liked was smitten with Miss Bridget?

Hours later, the very notion that Miriam might be behind the stolen brooch sent a shudder of dread down her spine. Especially when she allowed herself to revisit the way the elderly woman had gotten so defensive when Hannah brought up the brooch while sitting on her porch. Maybe it wasn't Michael's guilt that Miriam was thinking of.

"Hannah, you're back."

Willing her body to relax, Hannah headed toward the information desk and the familiar face of the head librarian. "Hi, Evangeline. It's good to see you again."

"Are you wanting to see more yearbooks?"

"Not this time. I was hoping I might be able to go through some newspapers from 1964 until about 1966? And, if you have them, old

Sunshine Club records that might show me who lived in a particular home in early 1966?"

"We have the club records, but they're kept in files in the back to protect privacy," Evangeline explained. "We typically ask patrons to write down the information they need, and we will get it to them within forty-eight hours. For you, though, I can try to compile it sooner—likely between this morning's story time and this afternoon's second-grade field trip." The librarian clapped a hand to her forehead. "Though I just remembered that I'm also teaching a computer-basics class to some senior citizens today. How did the day get so busy?"

"I can't tell you how many times that's happened to me, and I've never been able to figure out how. It's as if the day has a mind of its own." Hannah accepted a form from Evangeline and quickly filled it out. "This isn't time-sensitive, so please don't stress yourself out getting to it. Thank you for whatever you can do."

Evangeline glanced at the address and requested date range and then set the form beside her computer keyboard. "Now, for the newspaper archives, are you after national papers or local?"

"Local."

"That's easy. Come with me." Evangeline hurried out from behind the desk and led Hannah toward the bank of computers. When they reached it, she pulled out a chair for Hannah and turned on its assigned machine.

"A regular computer?" Hannah asked. "I grew up hearing about microfilm machines for this kind of stuff."

When the screen came to life, Evangeline tapped in a few words and then stepped back. "That's the way it was in the past, but many libraries have digitized newspaper collections nowadays. That way, patrons can search through all sorts of digital archives and databases. You don't need to worry about another patron having the materials you want to reference, and this method features keyword searches—something that wasn't possible in the days of microfilm and microfiche."

"Meaning I can type in an address and see if something comes up about it during the time frame I'm interested in?" Hannah asked.

"It's possible, though in my experience, addresses are only given in certain sections of newspapers, like the crime beat and real estate. News and feature articles tend to simply identify people as a resident of whatever town they're from."

"Right. That makes sense." She noted the year in the masthead of the 1960s-era version of the *Blackberry Valley Chronicle*: 1966. "And if I want to go on to a different issue, how do I do that?"

Evangeline pointed at the screen. "You click the back button here, or you can close out and move on, one by one, to each of the subsequent issues."

Hannah nodded. "Perfect."

Evangeline glanced at the wall clock. "If you're all set, I'll see what I can get done on your information request before this morning's story time participants begin arriving."

Hannah smiled up at Evangeline. "Thank you. And no rush on the records. I know you're busy."

After the librarian left, Hannah reached into the tote bag at her feet, plucked out her notepad and pen, and set them on the table to the right of the computer. Then she got to work, clicking, scrolling, occasionally typing, and clicking some more. Slowly but surely, she made her way through editions of the local weekly paper, starting at the beginning of 1964.

She scrolled past advertisements—including numerous ones for Dave's—and through reports of town meetings, stories about various school events and happenings, wedding announcements, obituaries, and hundreds of stand-alone photos with explanatory captions.

She stopped her search when she came across a smaller version of the very same wedding picture she'd seen in Miriam's home countless times from the early part of 1966. Clearly taken the moment Miriam and Michael had begun their walk down the church aisle as an officially married couple, the image captured their happiness as well as their hope for the future. She paused to read the details of the big day that accompanied the photograph and then began scrolling again, stopping to click in and out of the next issue and the one after that as her thoughts returned to the idea of Miriam having stolen the—

Her finger froze on the mouse as her gaze landed on a black-and-white picture of what she instantly recognized as Miriam Spencer's house. Below it were the words *For Sale*.

"So this is when you bought your house," Hannah murmured as she took in the written details of the home before returning her gaze to the picture.

The house itself had changed little in the years since the notice had been placed in the paper. She imagined how the wide front porch had spoken to Miriam as a young newlywed and wondered how long she had waited before adding her beloved rocking chairs. She silently applauded her friend's decision to put in the eastern redbud trees that blossomed so beautifully.

Hannah sat up straight, her gaze moving between the treeless land and the empty porch as she mentally compared the image in front of her to the one she'd seen in Penelope McIntosh's bag. At the time, Hannah hadn't paid much attention to the differences between Penelope's photo and how the house usually looked. She had assumed she couldn't see the trees because of the angle used to take the picture and had chalked up the empty front porch to a cleaning session. She'd barely noticed that it was black and white, assuming the photo had been taken with some kind of popular filter.

But the newspaper photo told her she'd been wrong. The picture was black and white because of its age, not because of any photo editing. The absence of the eastern redbud trees wasn't because of a camera angle—it was because they hadn't been planted yet. And the lack of furniture on the front porch wasn't because of a recent cleaning or staining. It was because Michael and Miriam Spencer did not yet own the house when the picture was taken.

That part made sense.

What didn't make sense was why Penelope had such an old photo of Miriam's house. The same Penelope who'd taken a job working inside this very home less than a month before, who'd stolen Miriam's vintage dresser set from a room that went on to be destroyed in a freak fire, and who'd claimed to have never heard of Blackberry Valley until she'd stood in front of a map, closed her eyes, and decided to find work in whatever town her finger landed on.

Hannah sat back in her chair, stunned.

The brooch had been stolen three years before the Spencers had purchased the house, which meant it could've already been under the floorboard when the old photo in the newspaper—and Penelope's bag—was taken.

"And the polishing part?" she whispered. "What better way to gain access than to be hired as a housekeeper and companion by the current owner?"

Hannah shoved her notepad and pen back into her bag and logged out of the computer.

The next stop on her day off was no longer Jump Start Coffee.

Chapter Twenty-Two

Grateful for the voice-activated system in her car that allowed her to place a call with her hands firmly on the steering wheel, Hannah waited through three rings before Lacy finally picked up.

"Hey, Hannah, are you on your way over? I made your favorite chicken pasta salad along with—get this—potato candy," Lacy said brightly, the bouncing of her voice telling Hannah that she was on the move. "I remember how much you used to love it. Whenever Mom made it for a family event at our house, we always knew the leftovers wouldn't survive your next visit."

The memory tickled at some corner of her brain, and Hannah did her best to muster up a little reciprocal enthusiasm. "It has peanut butter in it, right? And powdered sugar?"

"It does."

"Oh yes, I remember that stuff quite fondly." Hannah turned onto a rural two-lane road that would take her from the downtown section of Blackberry Valley to Lacy's farm. She carefully shifted the conversation toward the topic that really interested her. "Did you have time to talk with Penelope this morning?"

"I did."

"And she told you about the vintage dresser set she took from Miriam's house before the fire?"

The movement she'd heard on Lacy's end of the call ceased in favor of a long, drawn-out exhale. "She did. And she feels awful about it."

"Do you think she feels that way because it was wrong, or because I caught her?" Hannah hated to phrase the question that way, but she needed Lacy's input on it.

"The former." A muted bleat in the background of the call and her friend's brisk tone meant Lacy was moving again. "From what I've been able to gather since she started working here, she doesn't have any family or friends to speak of. She simply closed her eyes, stood in front of a map, and—"

"Pointed to Blackberry Valley, Kentucky," Hannah finished for her friend. "As if it was fate."

The bleat grew louder, more insistent. "You okay, Hannah? I'm getting the sense that maybe you woke up on the wrong side of the bed or something."

She took a right at an intersection. "I'm sorry. I don't mean to sound like that. I'm just on edge, I guess."

"I can understand that. Penelope tried to steal something from Miriam, who is our friend."

"She didn't *try* to steal something, Lacy. She *did* steal something."

"Yes, but she gave it back, didn't she?"

"*After* I confronted her."

"Hannah, this isn't like you. You're usually much more forgiving than this."

"I know. But I think that, in this situation, there's more."

"What kind of 'more'?" Lacy asked.

Hannah slowed for the last bend in the road before Lacy's farm, taking in the sunflowers in the meadow bending toward the sun. "I came across something this morning that might disprove Penelope's story about how she decided to come to Blackberry Valley."

"What are you talking about?" Lacy asked.

"Remember on Saturday, when I offered to take her picture with Mimi and the kids, and I got her phone from her bag?"

"I do."

"Well, Rocky had tipped over the bag, and some of its contents spilled out. I picked up her things and put them back in the bag, and that's when I saw that she had three photographs in there," Hannah explained. "One was of Miriam sitting on a porch rocking chair, which I thought was sweet. Another showed the guest room before the fire and before Penelope stole Miriam's dresser set, and the third was a black-and-white shot of the exterior of Miriam's house. That last one was likely taken in or before 1966. As in before Michael and Miriam moved in."

"Okay, so?" Lacy asked. "I don't understand why that would mean Penelope is lying about how she came to town."

"Lacy, think about why she'd have a decades-old photo of a house she's never lived in. I think she knew about Blackberry Valley and intentionally chose to come here. And I don't believe she came to work for Miriam by happenstance."

"What are you saying, Hannah?" Lacy asked. "Do you think she started the fire at Miriam's house?"

"No. That's the one thing I *don't* think she did."

"Why not?" Lacy asked.

"Because I asked her about it."

"But if you think she's been untruthful about everything else, why not the fire too?"

"Aside from the fact that the authorities say it was an accident, I saw her reaction, and I don't think she was faking it. She was appalled at the idea that anyone could think she'd done that. Maybe it's what you said in the beginning about her still being here rather than taking off afterward. Or maybe I'm just being horribly naive, and I'll end up eating my words. But whatever the case, my gut tells me she didn't start it." Hannah slowed at the approach to the gravel parking area outside Lacy's barn and carefully pulled to a stop as Hennifer dashed across the drive in front of her. "If she was involved with the fire at all, I think it must have been an accident. Maybe she happened to set the mirror at exactly the wrong angle when she cleaned in there. But I don't think it was premeditated."

"Phew."

"However, her pretending she's never heard of Blackberry Valley? I'm no longer buying *that* story."

"Because of the picture of Miriam's house you saw in her bag?" There was no denying the skepticism in Lacy's tone.

"Because of the *vintage* photo of Miriam's house that I saw in her bag." Hannah put the car in park. "Anyway, I'm here now. I'm guessing you're in the barn?"

"I am."

"I'll be there in a minute. But before we eat, I really need to talk to Penelope."

"Penelope isn't here," Lacy said.

Hannah startled. "What do you mean she's not here? You said she came clean to you about Miriam's dresser set."

"She did—when she called early this morning to say she wasn't coming in today, after all."

"But she practically begged you to let her come in today," Hannah said.

"I know, but I guess she changed her mind."

Hannah forced herself to take a deep breath and let it out slowly as she tried to gather her thoughts. "Did she happen to say *why* she wasn't coming in? What she planned to do instead?"

"She said she had some making up to do where Miriam was concerned."

"Meaning?" Hannah asked.

"She said she wanted to spend the day doing stuff for her for free."

Alarm bells clanged in her head. Penelope had already stolen from Miriam once, and Hannah suspected that there was plenty the young woman wasn't telling them.

She made sure there were no loose animals around her vehicle then threw the Outback into reverse. "I'm sorry, Lacy, but I'm going to have to take a rain check on the food and our time together."

"Why? You're right outside the barn, aren't you?"

She floored it toward the main road. "Not anymore. I'm on the way to Miriam's. I'll call you later."

Miriam was on her front porch with a tall glass of lemonade and a book when Hannah parked in front of the house. When she climbed out of the car, she could hear a vacuum cleaner through the screen door.

Penelope.

Hiking the strap of her tote bag higher on her shoulder, Hannah hurried up the flagstone walkway and onto the porch.

"Hannah!" Miriam said in surprise. "You're back."

She found a smile for her friend, only to feel it slip from her face as the vacuum cleaner went silent. "I take it that's Penelope inside?"

"She wants to make things right," Miriam said. "Something she really doesn't have to do now that she's returned my dresser set. But I can understand how she might want to do this so she can forgive herself."

It was on the tip of her tongue to argue the point, but Hannah let it go and pointed into the house. "I need to talk to Penelope, Miriam. It can't wait."

"Is there a problem, dear?"

"I'm not sure."

Slowly, Miriam set down her glass. "I'm coming with you then."

"No. Please, Miriam. I can do this alone. If it goes the way I suspect it will, then I'll bring you in on it."

"This is my house," Miriam said firmly. "I'm coming *now*."

Hannah knew better than to continue the argument. She opened the door, held it for Miriam to walk through, and then let it bang in their wake as she joined her friend on their way to the living room.

"Penelope, dear?" Miriam called out. "Can you please come in here for a moment?"

"Of course. I'll be right there." Moments later, the tall blond strode into the room and stopped dead, nearly dropping the dustcloth she held. "Hannah? What are you doing here? Is something wrong, Miss Miriam?"

Hannah said, "I need to ask you a few questions, Penelope."

"Why don't we all sit down?" Miriam suggested.

"Okay." Penelope perched on the sofa, and Miriam took a seat beside her.

Hannah remained standing and propped her hands on her hips. "I need you to be honest, Penelope. You didn't really come here because you closed your eyes and pointed at Blackberry Valley on a map, did you? And you showing up at Miriam's asking for work wasn't a coincidence either, was it?"

Gasping, Miriam clasped her hands together. "What are you saying, Hannah?"

"Do you want to tell her, Penelope, or should I?" Hannah asked.

"Tell her what?" Penelope whispered.

"About whatever your history is with this house."

Miriam's gaze shot first to Hannah then to Penelope. "You have a connection to my house?"

Penelope swallowed hard. "I…" She lowered her head and bit her lip.

"We're listening," Hannah said, not unkindly.

Penelope took a deep breath then fixed her gaze on the far wall. "My mother was born in this house the same year you moved in, Miss Miriam."

"I remember there was a baby who'd been born a few months before Michael and I bought the house. We felt bad that the family had to pack up a newborn for us to move in. The baby was your mother?" Miriam's eyes widened, and she sat up straighter. "That's why you took the dresser set, isn't it? Because when I told you how it had been left behind by the previous owner, you realized it belonged to your grandmother?"

Penelope wrung the dustcloth in her lap. "I know that wasn't reason enough to take it without asking. I don't mean this as an excuse, but my parents were killed in a car accident earlier this year, and my grandparents are long gone. I have no siblings, no other relatives. Even the childhood home I grew up in, with all of them around me, is gone. In its place is a veterinary clinic."

"How sad," Miriam said gently.

"I felt like I no longer had any sort of real connection to my family. So when I came across a picture of this house and read my grandmother's diary entry about how much she loved it in the relatively short time they'd rented it, I wanted to see it for myself. See if I could feel close to her and my grandfather, and maybe even my mother a little too." Tears started running down Penelope's cheeks. "I just miss my family so much and wanted some way to connect with them, but I shouldn't have hurt someone who was so kind to me."

Miriam pulled Penelope close and scowled at Hannah over the top of her head. "Hannah, I think you should go. You've upset Penelope enough."

Penelope straightened and shook her head. "No, Miss Miriam. Hannah is right to be here. She's watching out for you because she cares about you. And she was right. I did lie about picking Blackberry Valley at random. I also stole your dresser set."

"Which actually belonged to your kin, and therefore by rights to you," Miriam pointed out.

Penelope gave her a small smile. "Thank you, but I should have told you the truth and simply asked you for it. Instead, I stole it and let you believe it burned in the fire. Even after you'd been so kind and welcoming to me, making me feel like I wasn't alone for the first time in months." Penelope gazed up at Hannah. "I'm sorry for all of it. I love it here. Everyone I've met has been so kind. I love working at the farm with Lacy, and I loved being part of those baby goats being born. I've looked at that picture you took for me more times than I can count, Hannah."

"People make mistakes," Miriam said, patting Penelope's hand. "The important thing is that you're owning up to all of them and doing your best to make it right."

"Is she, though?" Hannah asked. "Is wanting a connection to your family really the only reason you sought out this house, Penelope?"

"She said that was the reason, dear," Miriam replied firmly as Penelope's cheeks grew pink.

Hannah kept her gaze firmly on the young woman beside Miriam. "I know that's what she said. I'm just asking if there's more."

"What else could there be?" Miriam asked.

Penelope avoided eye contact with either of them.

Hannah crouched to peer into Penelope's face. "Perhaps she was searching for something in particular?"

"What on earth could she have…" Miriam's voice trailed off, and she suddenly twisted to face Penelope. "Are *you* the one who polished the ruby brooch?"

Penelope raised her head and gaped at them, clearly dumbfounded. "Is *that* what the treasure was?" she asked. "A ruby brooch?"

Swiping away the remnants of her tears, Penelope pushed off the couch and hurried over to her bag. She loosened the drawstring, rummaged around inside it for what felt to Hannah like an eternity, and pulled out a folded piece of yellowed paper.

"I found this drawing with the picture of the house." Penelope unfolded the paper and carried it back to Hannah. "I thought it was a treasure map, but then, when I got here, it made no sense."

Hannah smoothed out the paper and then held it up for better inspection. Sure enough, a small X appeared inside a tiny square—a square that didn't fit with the room in which she stood. She studied the crude drawing. "What is this?"

"I thought it was a sketch of the inside of this house." Penelope opened her arms to the space around them. "And that it was going to lead me to something my grandparents had left behind. But clearly my imagination ran away with me. I feel kind of silly about it."

Hannah studied the X and the oddly shaped squares and rectangles around it before handing the paper to Miriam. "Does this make sense to you? And what is that?" She'd caught a glimpse of three tiny words scrawled on the back of the page.

Miriam flipped the paper over. "It says, 'I am sorry.'"

"Are you sure?" Hannah asked.

"That was how I read it too," Penelope said.

Miriam stared down at the drawing for several long moments. Finally, she tapped the X in the center. "This would be right for where you found the ruby brooch, Hannah."

She stared at her elderly friend. "How can you tell?"

"The house is laid out differently now than it was when we bought it. This room was actually a small bedroom with an oddly placed closet in the center. Michael was quite handy, and he decided to remove the closet. He also took down one of the bedroom walls to make the living room the size it is now," Miriam said.

"How did you not find the brooch then? The floors would have been ripped up, right?"

Miriam smiled. "Michael wanted to, but I loved the floors, squeaks and all. So he simply patched where he had to and left everything else as it was."

"So since this paper was in with Penelope's grandparents' things, one or both of them might have been behind the theft of Miss Bridget's ruby brooch," Hannah said. "But how would they have managed it?"

"I know I haven't given the best representation of my family, but I can assure you my grandparents weren't like that," Penelope protested.

"I'm not sure who else it could be," Hannah said, trying to keep her tone gentle.

"Actually, there might be another explanation." Miriam studied the crude map, pressing her fingertips to her lips. "This was with their things, yes?"

Penelope nodded.

"The *X* in this drawing is that spot there," Miriam said, pointing at the floor. "Where Hannah found a brooch that was stolen sixty years ago."

"And freshly polished by someone," Hannah said.

"That wasn't me," Penelope insisted. "I promise it wasn't, Miss Miriam."

Every rational thought in Hannah's head told her that couldn't be true—that Penelope had the map and had found a way to get herself into Miriam's house.

Yet, even with all of that, she couldn't help but feel that Penelope was finally telling the truth. But who else could have known about and had access to the brooch? And why did they intentionally leave it under a floorboard in someone else's house?

It made no sense, no matter how she examined it.

A sudden vibration from her back pocket made her pull out her phone. She checked the display then held up a finger to Miriam and Penelope as she answered the call. "Hello?"

"Hi, Hannah. This is Evangeline at the library."

"Hi, Evangeline." Hannah watched Penelope slump onto the couch beside Miriam and rest her head on the elderly woman's shoulder. Miriam patted her hand, murmuring words of encouragement.

"I've pulled together the information you asked for. You can pick it up anytime between now and closing, or at your earliest convenience tomorrow. It doesn't mean anything to me, but I hope it'll answer your question."

As Hannah watched an elderly woman comforting a young one who'd lied to and stolen from her, she wasn't sure that all her questions would ever be answered. But she was sure she was learning a lesson in forgiveness and second chances.

Chapter Twenty-Three

Hannah sat in the parking lot of Blackberry Valley Motor Lodge with a heavy heart long after Penelope had gotten out of the car and disappeared through a door. Because even though Hannah was glad to have at least a partial answer about the stolen brooch, she couldn't deny feeling bad for the young woman.

Was it wrong that Penelope had stolen from Miriam? Yes.

Was it wrong that Penelope had lied numerous times? Yes.

But to find out that the grandparents she'd been so desperate to have a connection with weren't who she'd grown up believing them to be was a pain Hannah could only imagine—one that surely explained the total silence in the car as she'd driven Penelope from Miriam's home to the motor lodge.

Hannah knew the pain of losing a mother. It weighed on her every day. But she still had her dad, Lacy, and the community she was slowly but surely reestablishing herself into now that she was back where she truly belonged.

Penelope, on the other hand, had nothing and no one. No support system to lean on in her overwhelming grief.

The ring of her phone filled the car's cabin. She checked the caller ID then answered. "Hey, Dad."

"What's wrong, sweetheart?"

Closing her eyes, she rested the back of her head against the seat. "How do you know there's something wrong?"

"I can hear it in your voice."

"All I said was, 'Hey, Dad.'"

"And that was enough. It was a very telling tone."

She sent up a silent prayer of thanks for the man on the other end of the call—a man who loved her unconditionally and was always, always there for her, no matter what. "Are you home right now?"

"Yes. Why?"

"I could use a hug."

"I think I can manage that."

She smiled in spite of the sadness she still felt. "I can't stay long though. I have to pick something up at the library that I requested yet don't really need anymore."

"Then why pick it up?" Dad asked.

"Because Evangeline went to the trouble of putting it together for me."

"I see. Where are you now?"

"In the parking lot of the motor lodge. I dropped someone off here—someone who worked for Miriam for a little while prior to the fire and now works for Lacy at the farm."

"Perfect. As luck would have it, I'm about halfway between where you are and the house. So I'll meet you there in a few minutes?"

"You bet."

Hannah slowly eased out of the parking lot and headed east. Before long, she turned into the driveway she knew so well, where her father stood awaiting her arrival. As wonderful as it felt to see him there, eager to give the hug she so desperately needed, her thoughts went to Penelope, who had no one to do the same for her. Who was in Penelope's corner?

She parked beside a tan-colored sedan, drew in a steadying breath, and exited the Outback into her father's waiting arms. For several long moments she simply let herself be held in his warm, strong embrace, soaking in the comfort of his unconditional love. "You have no idea how badly I needed that, Dad. Thank you so much."

"Anytime, Hannah. You're so grown up and independent, but it's nice to still be needed sometimes."

She gave his cheek a peck. "I'll always need my dad."

A loud thump from somewhere over her left shoulder pulled her attention toward the oversize shed her father had turned into a workshop when Hannah was ten years old. An even louder, heavier thump followed, and then a loud apology.

"No worries. It's fine. Really," replied a voice Hannah recognized as belonging to her uncle Gordon.

"What's going on in there?" she asked.

"Your uncle and Bruce are trying to build a pretty elaborate birdhouse for an outdoor market they want us to have a table at next month."

"How exciting. That sounds great, Dad."

"I agree, but it means we have a lot of work to do between now and then if we're going to have handcrafted things for people to buy."

Another thump, another string of apologies, and another reassurance from her uncle drew her attention back to the workshop door. "I'm guessing Bruce is dropping stuff?"

"It's like I told you the other day," Dad said. "His arthritis has gotten so bad he can't hold tools—or really anything that requires a grip—for long. And if he gets flustered or frustrated, as he does when his head *thinks* he can still do something his hands can no longer do, he starts dropping everything."

"That's sad."

"It is. But there are other ways he can help. He merely needs to realize that, and then everything will be fine." Dad walked over to a box on the ground next to the front steps of the house, carried it back to Hannah, and then set it on the hood of her car. "The reason I called you when I did was because I have one more thing to give to you for the restaurant. I've been working on it for a while, but I didn't want to say anything until I knew I could pull it off."

"What is it?" she asked.

"Open it and find out," Dad said, chuckling. "But be careful. I can help you get it out if you want."

Hannah stepped up to the box, slowly removed the lid, and stared down at the top of a piece of wood. "Is this another lid?"

"Why don't you take out the whole thing and see for yourself?"

She carefully obeyed—and gasped at the sight of an old-fashioned fire station…in miniature.

On one side of the two-truck bay was a miniature truck. Behind the empty bay, she spotted the classic fireman's pole. Beside the truck hung miniature firefighter coats above miniature boots. And beside those sat a tiny figurine that looked a lot like Smoky, the firehouse dog. Upstairs, on the second floor, were miniature beds, some neatly made, one rumpled as if the previous occupant had just left it to fight a fire.

"Dad," she whispered, her voice thick with emotion. "You made this? For me?"

"I did."

"This must have taken you forever. When did you start it?"

"The day you signed the papers on the old firehouse."

Again, she stared at the tiny firehouse, every miniscule detail perfect. "The coats and the boots are so tiny. How did you do that?"

"Trial and error, but mostly glue," he said, laughing. "And prayer. Lots and lots of prayer. Don't look too close, or you might not be so impressed."

"Oh, I'm impressed—trust me. It's absolutely perfect," she insisted. "And I know exactly where I'm going to put this in the restaurant. Low enough for people to see but high enough the little ones can't touch it."

"Good idea."

"Did Uncle Gordon help?"

"He listened as I tried to figure out all the different parts, sharing his thoughts from time to time. Especially about the pole, which stumped me for a little while. And Bruce was the one who came up with the idea of adding the dog. But since I did all the building, I alone am at fault if anything looks silly or doesn't hold up."

She watched as he closed the top on the miniature firehouse and then ran her fingers along one edge. "It's amazing, Dad. I absolutely love it."

"I'm glad. Now I'll box it back up, put it on the floor of your car, and let you get on your way before the library closes."

She held her arms open. "Another hug first. This time, though, it's for you."

"Hannah, every hug I get from you is for me, no matter the reason," he said, enveloping her in his arms. "I love you, kiddo."

"I love you too, Dad."

While Hannah still had no answers about the brooch under Miriam's floorboard, there was no denying the pick-me-up she'd gotten from her quick visit with her father. The miniature firehouse was partially responsible for the smile she wore on her way to the library, but even more so were his hugs, which reminded her that he always had her back.

Slowly, she made her way up the same flight of stone steps she'd walked mere hours before. Only this time, instead of questions for which she sought an answer, she had an answer that had left yet another question—one she knew in her heart that Evangeline and her data wouldn't be able to help with.

At the end of the day, the Berthold family brooch was no longer missing. And while she would never know how or why Penelope's grandparents had taken it, the crude treasure map seemed to prove that they had, and the apology written across the back pointed toward at least *some* remorse.

The only questions that still niggled at her thoughts were who had known the brooch was there all this time, and why had they bothered to polish it? The fact that Miriam was the only one who made sense for that part didn't escape Hannah. Especially in light of the unmistakable relief on the woman's face when it became obvious that the brooch had been hidden *before* she and Michael had purchased the house. That effectively cleared Michael of the theft. Hannah suspected that Miriam hadn't been completely certain of his innocence.

That would give Miriam a motive to keep the brooch looking perfect all these years. Even after Michael's death, Miriam's need to protect her husband's good name would have been paramount. And perhaps on some level, caring for the brooch might have provided a way for her to feel connected to Michael, as the house was a way for Penelope to feel connected to her own kin.

Then again, if maintaining a sense of connection with kin could be a motive for Miriam to have cared for the brooch, could Hannah continue to dismiss Tom as a suspect simply because he hadn't opted to sell the brooch as she would have expected, considering he was strapped for cash? Perhaps in this situation the brooch's sentimental value would have been greater than its monetary value for Tom and he'd done the polishing but just hadn't owned up for whatever reason.

Hannah shook off such thoughts as she stepped through the library's front door. The comforting smell of old books quieted her mind as she headed for the information desk and the woman who stood behind it, keying something into a computer.

"Do you ever take a break?" she asked by way of a greeting.

Evangeline chuckled. "If I need one. But it's always more interesting to do the things that need to be done around here."

"I appreciate you turning around my information request quicker than you needed to," Hannah said.

"It was my pleasure." Evangeline hopped off her stool, bent down behind the information desk, and reappeared with a manila envelope bearing Hannah's name in black ink. "Here you go. I compiled as much information as I could on the address you requested. When you're done with it, I ask that you either shred it yourself or bring it back to me to be shredded."

Hannah accepted the folder, though she was confident she no longer needed its contents. But it would have been rude to tell the head librarian so when she'd prioritized the request despite her busy day. "Thank you, Evangeline. I really appreciate it. And I'll return it to you when I'm done. Maybe even later today before you close."

Evangeline waved away her words with a neatly manicured hand. "You don't need to rush, Hannah. I know it's your day off from the restaurant. You don't need to be trekking back and forth to the library."

"It's a short walk," Hannah protested. "I can handle a 'trek' like that."

"I'm sure you can. But just take it home with you now, review it at your leisure, and bring it back when it's convenient."

"If you're sure. Thank you again." Hannah tucked the envelope under her arm and strolled out of the library, reflecting that even though she was unlikely to learn anything new, at least the records might make for some interesting reading.

Chapter Twenty-Four

Step by step, Hannah made her way through her favorite recipe for pepper steak stir-fry. She measured, chopped, sautéed, and mixed, appreciating how easy the dish was to customize for a single diner. On a whim, she tried a couple new touches, playing with the seasoning as well as the texture of the sauce. As she exercised her creative muscles, she felt the tension of the day finally release its grip on her body and her spirit.

Cooking had been that place of solace in her life from the moment she'd been able to climb onto a step stool and peer over the kitchen counter. Back then, she'd been content to do anything her mother had allowed—gather ingredients, pour something into a bowl, help hold the hand mixer. As she'd gotten older and been able to take on more tasks, her love of everything cooking-related grew and grew until she knew beyond a shadow of a doubt that she wanted to own her own restaurant one day. Between the meditative actions of preparing food, the sense of satisfaction at turning individual ingredients into a delicious meal, and the sense of connection to her mom, the kitchen had become Hannah's haven.

Now, after more than a decade spent learning every aspect of the business from waitstaff to kitchen to management in some of California's most acclaimed restaurants, she was exactly where she wanted to be, doing exactly what she'd always wanted. Did she get to spend as much time in the Hot Spot's kitchen as she sometimes wished? No. Owning a restaurant was about so much more than that. But she had the final say on every menu item, she was ready and able to cover Jacob on a moment's notice, and she had two days off a week in which she could cook to her heart's content, either to try out possible new recipes for the restaurant, or—as was the case at the moment—to work through something that was troubling her.

With a practiced hand, she spooned savory chunks of steak with crisp-tender onions and bell peppers over the hearty brown rice already on her plate, garnished it with fresh chives for an earthy sharpness, sprinkled fresh microgreens around the edges, and carried it to the place setting at her small kitchen table. She sat down, spread her napkin across her lap, reached for her fork—and stopped as her gaze came to rest on the unopened manila envelope to the right of her water glass.

Her sense of smell told her to wait to open it. The rumble in her stomach echoed the sentiment. Her finally relaxed neck and shoulders begged her to be reasonable.

Because what was the point in letting her meal go cold when she already knew who the previous occupants of Miriam's house had been, thanks to the confrontation with Penelope? There was no point.

She picked up her fork, slid its tines into a small piece of beef and a little bit of the pepper...and set it down on the edge of her plate in favor of the envelope, shaking her head at herself as she did.

She opened the envelope and pulled out three pages, stapled neatly together. The first page read:

July 1966
3 Cobbler Way
Blackberry Valley, KY
Current residents: Archie Norton (35); Abigail Norton (33)
Children: Female, Theresa (Born: May 4, 1966)

She reached across the packet for a sip of ice water, popped the waiting forkful of her meal into her mouth, and savored it for a moment, making a mental note of which changes she'd made to the dish had and hadn't worked. Then she continued reading.

Occupations: Archie, Teacher; Abigail, Homemaker
Owners: Jeremiah Davidson (40); Elizabeth Davidson (died Nov. 16, 1963)
Children: Male, Jeremiah B. (Born: March 1, 1955)

"Owner?" She stared at the page. The owners and the residents were separate families?

Her confusion faded as she remembered what Penelope had said about the photo of Miriam's house. Penelope had read her grandmother's diary entry about how much she'd loved the house for the short time they'd...

"Rented," she whispered. "Penelope said her grandparents rented the house. They never owned it."

Another, different tale began to form in her mind. She jumped up and raced around her couch for the leather-bound journal on top of her stack of paperback mystery novels. Flipping back the cover, she hastily thumbed her way to the last entry she'd read—the one dated June 12, 1964.

She skimmed her way through the first few paragraphs, stopping to read as she found the section she was searching for.

> Since neither Patrick nor I have any little boys in our families, we didn't know who could be the ring bearer. And then on a picnic last week, Patrick came up with the idea of asking Jerry. Even though it had been months since I'd seen Jerry, I knew he was the perfect choice—both because of the bond we created during his mother's illness, and as something happy for him to look forward to.
>
> But when I went in search of his father, I discovered that they've rented out their home and moved away. I'll miss my quiet talks and hugs from Jerry, but I pray that he and his father find their way through the pain and grief of the past year.

She read it again and again, the word *rented* gaining significance each time she did.

Then, on a hunch, she turned back to another entry.

> I saw Jerry today. His mother's birthday was yesterday. He wanted to tell me about the cake he helped make for her, a cake she ended up being unable to eat because of how sick she is.
>
> My heart aches for Libby, for her husband, and most especially for little Jerry. He wants her to walk him home from school the way she did before she got sick. He wants her to "laugh from her belly" at his jokes again. He wants to see her get

dressed up in her prettiest dress for a special dinner with his dad like she used to. And he wants her to hug him really tight again.

I don't know what to say to him when he says those things. So I pray with him instead. Patrick says God will watch over Jerry and his parents, and I know he's right.

"Jerry," she whispered. "Short for Jeremiah."

Was it possible? Someone connected both to Miss Bridget and Miriam's house?

Had Jerry somehow gotten Miss Bridget's brooch and hidden it under a floorboard in his home?

She thought about the almost treasure map-style paper Penelope had found in her grandmother's things—a woman who'd rented the house Jerry had lived in with his father and mother.

She considered the *I am sorry* written across the back and realized that what she'd seen as sloppy was more likely the work of a distraught child overcome by guilt.

Was this it? Had she found the real culprit behind Miss Bridget's stolen brooch?

Hannah hurried to the table and the packet Evangeline had put together. She skimmed the page until she got to the name listed as owner.

"Davidson." She tapped the paper. "I've heard that name recently, but where? Was it the restaurant? The firehouse? The—"

She sat up straighter. She knew where she'd heard it.

She pounced on the phone she'd left on the counter beside the sink and quickly scrolled through her contact list until she came to her father's name.

Chapter Twenty-Five

For the second time that day, Hannah pulled into her childhood driveway and stopped beside the tan-colored sedan she was getting used to seeing there. She shifted into park, turned off the engine, and silently waffled over the best prayer to make in that moment.

Did she pray that she was wrong and continue searching for the truth?

Or did she pray that she was right so Liam and his grandfather could finally know what had happened to Miss Bridget's brooch and why?

Glancing first at the house and then at the car parked beside her own, she murmured, "Dear Lord, let Your will be done. Guide me to handle this in the way You see fit."

She glanced at the house again to find her father making his way toward her. When he reached her Outback, she stepped out to greet him and welcomed yet another, even more-needed hug.

"I did as you asked and didn't tell Gordon and Bruce that you were on your way over, but I'd be lying if I didn't tell you my antennae are up," Dad said, releasing her from his embrace. "I know that when you left here this afternoon, you were looking forward to an evening where you didn't have to go anywhere or do anything besides read more of Miss Bridget's journal. So what's going on?"

She leaned back against her car. "Do you know if Bruce has a brother? Maybe one close to his age?"

"I don't know, but I could ask."

"Actually, no." She held up her hands. "It couldn't be a brother—there were no siblings listed. But maybe a cousin?"

Dad's brow lifted. "Why are you asking about Bruce's family?"

"You said he lived in town when he was little, right?"

"I think he said he was eight—maybe nine—when he moved out of Blackberry Valley. Why?"

"And his last name is Davidson, right?" Hannah pushed off the Outback and went over to peer through the windows of the sedan.

"That's right." Dad's tone was still puzzled.

She took in the steering wheel, the toolbox in front of the passenger seat, and a pry bar on the floor in the back. "Maybe I could ask him if he has a cousin around his age who lived in Blackberry Valley when he did."

"I'm sure you could. But why the interest?"

"Because if he does, and the cousin's name is Jeremiah, I'd like to talk to him."

"Actually, Bruce's name is Jeremiah," Dad said.

Hannah's gaze flew to her father. "What?"

"Yeah, I caught a glimpse of his driver's license when he paid for dinner once. I guess it's his legal first name. I asked him why he didn't go by that or Jerry, and he got so upset. Said anyone who was a friend called him Bruce, though he didn't go into why. So I call him Bruce. Gordon went through a phase where he didn't like his first name either, so I figured it was something like that, only Bruce didn't outgrow it like Gordon did."

Swallowing, she looked at the pry bar, suddenly seeing it in a different light. "Do you know anything about his background?"

"I don't make a habit of performing background checks on my friends. Now that's quite enough of the secrecy, Hannah." Dad wasn't often stern, so when he was, she tended to listen. "Why all these questions about Bruce? Is there an issue I need to be aware of?"

"I hate keeping things from you, but this isn't my story to tell. All I can say for now is that I need to talk to him. Alone."

If she had her way, her father and her uncle would be in the workshop on the other side of the driveway rather than on the front porch where they might overhear something Bruce wasn't ready for them to hear. But, then again, who knew how a person might react to having a decades' old secret come to light? Perhaps it was better for everyone that they were near enough to intervene if he needed them.

In the living room minutes later, Bruce sat on the couch, watching her with a curious expression. "What can I do for you, Hannah?"

Her palms suddenly clammy, Hannah crossed to the fireplace, took the picture from her parents' wedding from the mantel, and handed it to Bruce. "Did you know my mom?"

"No."

"She was my everything," Hannah said around the rising lump in her throat. "Our family was always close, and I don't know where I'd be without my dad. But the relationship I had with my mom was truly special. So much of who I am is tied to her, and now that I'm back in Blackberry Valley, I see and feel her everywhere. The memories have been almost overwhelming."

"I'm sorry for your loss." Bruce held the picture out to her. When she didn't take it immediately, he dropped it onto the couch beside him as if it were a hot potato.

"Your mom called you Jerry, didn't she, Bruce? And you were just a child when she passed. That's so young. I was an adult when I lost my mom, and I still felt like I was too young to handle something like that."

Bruce's gaze snapped to hers, but he didn't reply. Somehow, his answering silence was deafening.

"I can't imagine how hard that must've been for you." She perched on the edge of the coffee table so she and Bruce were facing each other at eye level. "But I'm glad you had Miss Bridget, and I know how much she cared about you."

His face drained of all color. He swallowed and dropped his hooded gaze to the floor between their feet.

"You took her brooch to give to your mom, didn't you?" she asked softly.

Perhaps it was the gentleness in her tone, or the years of built-up secrets—or both—but Bruce finally spoke as if a dam had burst inside him. "I wanted her to smile one last time," he whispered. "But she died before I could give it to her."

Hannah laid a hand on his.

He rubbed his free hand over his face. "And then I was too afraid to give it back, so I hid it in the compartment my mom made for me under the floorboard." He gave Hannah a sad smile. "Like so many little boys, I had a pirate phase, and Mom called that my treasure chest. Only she and I knew about it. Before I could figure out how to give the brooch back to Miss Bridget, Dad was packing us up to move."

"So you made a map and wrote an apology, hoping someone would figure it out."

He gaped at Hannah. "You found that?"

"The people who rented your house found the map, but not the brooch. I don't know if they didn't realize it was a map, or if it got mixed up with their things during their move and they only discovered it after they'd left. Either way, it seems they didn't actually use it. So you were still the one person who knew where the brooch was." She gave him a moment to process before continuing. "You recently went into the house and polished it, didn't you?"

He pushed off the couch and slowly made his way over to the window beside the fireplace. "I've wondered whether the brooch was still there ever since I came back to Blackberry Valley. A few weeks ago, I started driving past the house, craving a connection with my mother. She missed most of my life. There was so much I never got to share with her, so many times I would have given anything to pour out my troubles to her and receive her comfort and advice. It hurt to see the place where she lived and died, but it helped me feel close to her somehow."

Hannah simply nodded. He didn't need her interrupting with questions. He needed someone to listen.

Bruce ran his fingers through his hair. "One day, I saw the woman who lives in the house leaving with a younger fellow, who carried a suitcase for her. That told me the house would be vacant for a little while. The next day, I saw a young woman hurry out through the back door, and I didn't think she'd taken the time to lock it. I was right."

Hannah nodded again, reflecting that must have been Penelope, rushing out of the house with the dresser set she'd taken.

"It took me another day to get up the courage to go inside. The house was different than I remembered as a kid, but I figured out pretty quickly where the brooch would be if it was still there. So I pulled up the board. I wanted to see it again. And I wanted to make it look the way it had when I had it in my pocket to show my mother. It would have made her smile. I know it. But like I said, when I went into her room with it, she was gone."

Hannah drew in a sharp inhale. What a horrible thing to happen to a little boy.

"While I was polishing it, it was as if I could feel my mother telling me to come clean, to take the brooch to the police and tell them what I'd done. But then I heard a car door slam outside, and I realized I smelled smoke. I got flustered and dropped the brooch into the box. Next thing I knew, I heard someone outside calling for help. I tried to put the lid on and move the floorboard back in place with these arthritic hands and get out of there before someone saw me."

She gasped. "You were in the house when the fire started?"

He must have misunderstood her tone of concern for one of suspicion, because he said quickly, "Yes, but I promise I didn't start it. I really, truly didn't. But then I did what I've done for so many years. I stayed silent. My mother would be ashamed of me."

"The fire was ruled an accident, and I don't believe for a second your mother wouldn't be proud of you. You're coming clean now," she said.

"I wish I could take credit for that, if for no other reason than to be the son my mom raised me to be, but you know I can't." He gave her a wry smile. "Who knows if I ever could have mustered the courage to confess if you hadn't come to ask me about it?"

"Maybe you wouldn't have. But if you're willing and able, I know who you can come clean to, and I have no doubt he will hear you with his ears *and* his heart."

Bruce hesitated, gazing out the window, then faced Hannah once more. "Miss Bridget's family, the Bertholds, right? I'd like that."

Hannah tapped on her phone's screen a few times and connected a call. When it was answered, she said, "Hello, Liam? Can we set up a get-together with your grandfather? A friend of mine needs to tell him something."

"He'll be delighted," the fire chief replied. "He loves you, and I'm sure he'll feel that any friend of yours is a friend of his. I'm seeing him tomorrow, so how about I call you then, and we can set it up?"

"That's perfect. Thanks, Liam. I'll talk to you later." She hung up and smiled at Bruce.

"Who was that?" he asked timidly.

"Fire Chief Liam Berthold, the grandson of Miss Bridget. His grandfather, Patrick, will be delighted to meet you," Hannah said. "No matter what you have to tell him."

"You may think I'm a coward, but would you be willing to come with me?" Bruce asked.

"There's nothing cowardly about needing a little emotional support," Hannah assured him. "I'll definitely be there."

Chapter Twenty-Six

Some days later, Hannah stood by the Hot Spot's hostess stand, taking in the hustle and bustle of her full restaurant. A distinct click broke through her thoughts.

"Did you just take a picture of me?" Hannah asked Liam as he lowered his phone and closed the gap between them in two long strides.

"I did."

"Any particular reason?"

Liam grinned at her. "You looked so happy standing there, I couldn't resist."

"I *am* happy," she said as, once again, she drank in the many faces she saw—people who'd welcomed her back to Blackberry Valley with open arms, and those she'd met recently yet felt as if she'd known far longer. "*Really* happy, in fact."

He pointed at the framed journal entry on the wall behind her head. "Speaking of happy, thank you for doing that. I've caught my grandfather glancing over at it at least a half dozen times since we got here."

She took in Miss Bridget's beautiful handwriting and heartfelt words, now preserved behind glass for all to see.

> *To love a firefighter is to love a hero.*
> *I thank the good Lord every day for mine.*

"I came across that the other night. As soon as I saw it, I knew that was the page to frame," she said. "I can't think of a more perfect way to sum up the theme here."

"I agree." He showed Hannah the photo he'd taken. "What were you thinking in that moment?"

She studied her father and her uncle at a table, laughing and smiling over some story from their youth, no doubt. At the next table over, Neil entwined his fingers with Lacy's, their bond after twelve years of marriage strong and evident.

"Do you have certain sounds you love to hear?" she asked in response.

Liam drew his head back. "I don't see how that answers my question, and I asked mine first."

She laughed. "Humor me."

He rubbed at the five o'clock shadow along his jawline, clearly considering her question. "I like the sound of the word *son* when my dad says it. I like the sound of the word *grandson* when my grandfather says it. And I like the sound of my guys' voices in the firehouse after a call because then I know everyone made it back safely. I can even tell how it went by their voices, even when I can't quite make out what they're saying."

"Those are good sounds for sure."

"And you?" he asked. "What are your favorite sounds, since you don't want to tell me what you were thinking?"

"Actually, that's exactly what I was thinking—about my favorite sounds." She rocked back on the heels of her sandals, returning Penelope's wave from the table she shared with Miriam. The two had truly formed a special connection, and she prayed that they continued to do each other good. "They're all right here, in this room."

"Which sounds would those be?"

"My dad's laugh, Elaine welcoming another customer, people talking about their day and sharing moments from their lives, the growing confidence in Dylan's voice as he becomes more comfortable at his job, the sound of Raquel's quiet squeal when she realizes Marshall Fredericks is sitting in her section again. The—"

"Wait. Marshall Fredericks? The food guy from the paper?"

Hannah nodded toward another table. "See for yourself."

"That's him all right. Raquel likes him?"

Hannah grinned. "She's not ready to admit it yet, but she does."

"And you're okay with him coming here after he dinged your restaurant?"

"More than okay. In fact, I ran into him briefly outside the library the other day and thanked him for what he wrote."

Liam stared at her. "You *thanked* him?"

She spread her hands toward the picture frames and displays hanging around the room. "Marshall did me a favor with what he said, Liam. It's made the Hot Spot even more special, more authentic. And it's how I've gotten to know you and your grandfather better. Marshall was the catalyst for all of that. My listening to his take has definitely improved the atmosphere in here."

"I think that's an amazing way to look at it," Liam told her, respect in his tone. "Any other favorite sounds?"

"So many. I love the sound of the bell that lets Raquel and Dylan know another order is ready. I love the sound of Jacob clattering around in the kitchen, whipping up his amazing food—food that he and I developed over months and months of work and are constantly fine tuning. I love the sound of *all* of it," Hannah told him. "This, right now, in this place? This is what a community is, Liam. It's the people. The camaraderie. The sharing. The love. And, in the case of your family and Bruce—*the forgiveness.*"

She directed his attention to the table he'd left to talk to her. There, engrossed in conversation, was Liam's grandfather and the man his beloved late wife had known and treasured as Jerry.

"Bruce was a little boy, facing unfathomable loss, when he took my grandmother's brooch. He didn't take it to hurt her—he took it in a young boy's attempt to fix the unfixable." Liam crossed his arms. "It's like my grandfather said when you brought Bruce out to speak to us. My grandmother would want us to forgive him, just as God would. And so, we do."

"But you're going one step further by sitting down to have dinner with him," Hannah said. "That's truly beautiful."

Liam shrugged, his ears growing a bit pink. "Sheriff Steele officially handed my grandmother's brooch back to my grandfather earlier this week—safe and sound. As my grandfather said, no harm, no foul."

"I'm glad."

"Me too." Liam returned Hannah's attention to his grandfather and Bruce. "And that's nothing you wouldn't have done. In fact, you're behind that."

"I haven't done anything," she protested.

"You created this place, Hannah. A place where the community you love so much can play out in real time, again and again." Liam tucked his phone into his pocket. "I'll text you the picture I just took of you. It's a keeper."

She blinked at him in surprise. "Why?"

"I felt drawn to take it because of your smile. I feel drawn to keep it for the same reason."

"I still don't understand."

"Well, you said the sounds of this place make you happy, right? I suppose I feel that if your joy in that moment spoke to me so strongly then, I'd like to keep it in case I need something like that in the future. Your joy here inspires me. I'd like it to continue doing so."

Hannah gazed around the restaurant—her restaurant. "I'd like that too, Liam. I pray the Hot Spot is around to inspire us all for a good, long time."

From the Author

Dear Reader,

I can't begin to tell you what an honor it was to write this kick-off book for the Mysteries of Blackberry Valley. The characters of Hannah, Liam, Lacy, Gabriel, and the rest of the residents I feature came alive for me in a way that made them feel like friends—friends I got to know better and better with each page I wrote.

That's what reading has always been for me—a chance to escape for a little while, a way to explore a new town or have a new adventure, and a place to make new friends—friends I look forward to visiting with again in each new book that follows.

I hope this series does the same for you.

Until next time, best wishes and happy reading!

Signed,
Laura Bradford

About the Author

While spending a rainy afternoon at a friend's house as a child, Laura Bradford fell in love with writing over a stack of blank paper, a box of crayons, and a freshly sharpened number-two pencil.

Today, Laura is the *USA Today* bestselling author of many cozy mystery series. She has also penned four Amish-based women's fiction novels set in and around Lancaster, Pennsylvania. When she's not writing, Laura loves to bake, travel, and advocate for those living with multiple sclerosis.

The Hot Spotlight

In the Mysteries of Blackberry Valley series, Hannah Prentiss has converted the town's old firehouse into her restaurant, the Hot Spot. As we see in this first book, she works hard to capitalize on the building's history in everything from her menu to the decorations on the wall.

Hannah's ability to see new purpose for an old firehouse is something that's played out in various places across the United States. Let's take a look at a few.

On Lafayette Street, on the edge of Chinatown in New York City, a gorgeous old firehouse has been converted into the well-known documentary production and film education center called DCTV.

In Los Angeles, California, the Old Plaza Firehouse was built in 1884 and served as a firehouse for the next thirteen years. More than fifty years later—after housing several businesses—the building was restored and still stands today as a firefighting museum, showcasing equipment and uniform pieces from the late nineteenth and early twentieth centuries.

In Silver Spring, Maryland, Fire Station 1 restaurant is located in a restored vintage firehouse. Part of the decor includes the front part of a fire truck, which is perfect for photo ops. Might be something fun for Hannah to consider integrating at the Hot Spot!

Perhaps one of the prettiest former firehouses can be found on East 4th Street in Duluth, Minnesota. Built in 1889, it served as one of the first fire stations in this town at a time when the city of Duluth moved from a volunteer to municipal fire department. Today, the building provides affordable housing to members of the community.

Maybe there's an old firehouse that's been repurposed into something else in your town or state, as well.

From the Hot Spot Kitchen

LACY'S MOTHER'S POTATO CANDY

Ingredients:

½ cup plain cooked and cooled mashed potatoes

½ cup softened salted butter

6–7 cups powdered sugar, plus additional for dusting

2 teaspoons vanilla extract

Creamy peanut butter

Directions:

Mix mashed potatoes, butter, and one cup of sugar in a large bowl. Use a hand mixer to mix until combined. Add remaining sugar, 1 cup at a time, mixing until combined. Check the consistency after adding 6 cups of powdered sugar. Dough should be moldable for rolling into ball shapes. If not, continue to add sugar in ¼ cup increments until moldable. Add vanilla extract.

Refrigerate dough 30 to 60 minutes. Dust your surface with powdered sugar. Divide chilled dough into two pieces. Roll into a rectangle about ¼ inch thick. If your dough is too sticky or falling apart, add more sugar, reshape into a ball, and return to refrigerator to cool.

Spread peanut butter over rectangle of dough, leaving a small edge on each side uncovered. Repeat with second piece. Roll the dough into a cylinder by using the longer side, as when making cinnamon rolls. Once rolled, cut in pieces around ½ inch wide.

Store in an airtight container for up to one week. When storing, use parchment paper between layers to prevent sticking.

Read on for a sneak peek of another exciting book in the *Mysteries of Blackberry Valley* series!

The Key Question
BY VIRGINIA SMITH & BETH ADAMS

Bright midday sunlight gleamed through the front windows of the Hot Spot, casting a soft golden glow around the dining room. Hannah Prentiss had spent the past hour sliding the updated menus into protective sleeves. It felt good to get that task done. Scanning the room, she saw a hundred other things that still required attention—the big plate-glass windows could be cleaned, the salt and pepper shakers should be refilled, the silverware needed to be rolled into napkins—but she had to get going.

She put away the menus at the hostess stand before walking through the dining room. She pushed open the double swinging doors that led to the restaurant's kitchen, which was situated in the back of the renovated firehouse. They were still several hours away from seating their first guests today, but on a sunny Saturday in July, Hannah expected a full house, and chef Jacob Forrest was already in the kitchen prepping for dinner.

"I'm headed over to Lacy's to talk about eggs," Hannah called.

Jacob gave her a thumbs-up. "I've got things under control here."

Hannah was grateful to have found a chef with so much experience here in Blackberry Valley, Kentucky. The Hot Spot was Hannah's restaurant, and she worked in the kitchen when needed, but she relied on Jacob's skill as a chef, which had earned them a loyal customer base within weeks of opening.

Hannah walked out into the sunshine, enjoying the warmth on her skin, and climbed into her Outback to head down Main Street. The little town of Blackberry Valley was always pretty with its quaint streets filled with cute shops and cafés, but the flags waving from lampposts for the recent Fourth of July parade were a nice addition. Beyond the little village, hills rose up all around them, covered in glorious green foliage. Sometimes, Hannah still couldn't believe she lived here. After so many years in Los Angeles, it felt like a dream to have come home again.

She smiled as she drove out of town and onto the rural road that wound past horse farms, with their stately fences surrounding open fields, and rows of corn, lush and green in the summer sun. She passed by the turnoff for the dirt road that led to the entrance of the limestone caves under the Bluegrass Hollow Farm cornfields, and then the barn, big and brilliantly red against the deep blue sky, and finally turned into the driveway that led to the pretty white farmhouse with the big front porch and black shutters.

Memories washed over her as she stood in front of the farmhouse she had visited so often as a teenager. How many sleepovers had she enjoyed with her best friend in this house? Her gaze rose to the window on the top floor, centered above the front door and nestled in the center of the steeply pitched roof. She and Lacy had spent hours talking on the seat in that window. That was no longer Lacy's bedroom, not since she and her husband, Neil, had accepted ownership of the farm from Lacy's widowed mother and moved down to the main floor.

A pair of horses stood at the wooden fence on the far side of the house, the grass in their pasture even greener than the one where the goats grazed. Their heads hung over the fence's top plank, their gazes fixed on Hannah.

"Hello, Stunner," she called in their direction. "Hello, Misty." She thought that was Razzle Dazzle over on the far side of the pasture.

As if they'd been waiting for her acknowledgment, they both tossed their heads before withdrawing from the fence.

"Hi, Hannah!" Lacy stepped out onto the porch in khaki cargo shorts, boots, and a T-shirt, her reddish-brown hair pulled back into a messy ponytail. "Good to see you."

"You too."

Lacy trotted down the steps and across the driveway to the mailbox on the side of the road. A hand-painted sign that said FARM-FRESH EGGS hung from the bottom of the mailbox. "I heard the mail truck go by a few minutes ago." She opened the little metal door and pulled out a stack of envelopes.

She led Hannah inside the house, which was blessedly cool. The shade from the trees around the house made it a respite on the hottest summer day. Lacy led her past the parlor, through the living room, where a half-done jigsaw puzzle waited on a side table, and into the kitchen.

Lacy gestured to the table. "Have a seat," she said. "Lemonade?" She set the stack of mail on the table next to a notebook, pen, and her phone.

"Please." Hannah sat down in a cane-bottom chair. The kitchen still had the same wooden cabinets that hung here when they were kids, but Lacy had painted them a grayish blue and had replaced the old laminate counter with butcher block.

Lacy set two glasses of cold lemonade on the table as she sat. "Let's talk eggs. I'm thrilled that your restaurant is doing so well you need more. Right now you're getting fifteen dozen a week. How many more do you need?"

Bluegrass Hollow Farm had been passed down through Lacy's family on her mother's side for generations. When Lacy's father, Frank, passed away, her mother, Christine, transferred the farm to her daughter. Lacy grew the farm's chicken business to a very profitable level, which had worked out well for Hannah. She was passionate about sourcing quality ingredients from local farms for the dishes at the Hot Spot, and Lacy had been supplying eggs since the restaurant opened.

Hannah took a sip of the lemonade. It was exactly the right combination of sweet and tart, and she was pretty sure Lacy had made it from scratch, judging by the flavor and the bowl of fresh lemons sitting on the counter. Hannah cocked her head as she considered the question. "Since I'm open five days a week, and only for dinner—"

"Which I still think is a mistake," Lacy interjected. "Blackberry Valley has no good place for brunch on Sundays. If you provided a local option, most people would stay in town rather than drive somewhere else."

"I would, but then I'd have to work every Sunday." Hannah shook her head. "I'd never be able to go to church, and that's important to me."

"There's that." Her friend tapped the pen on her notebook. "So, how many more eggs?"

Hannah took another sip of her lemonade and thought through the list of current offerings. The Hot Spot's menu would change with the seasons, since she planned on using locally grown produce whenever she could. Kentucky's vegetable offerings in early July were plentiful and diverse, which meant the new menu brimmed with variety.

"I use them in desserts, of course. And in the breading for the chicken tenders." She used her fingers to tick off items. "Some of the salads have them. And I use egg yolks in my béchamel sauce, which technically makes it the Greek version called *besamel*."

"No kidding?" Lacy cast a grin her way. "No wonder your Hot Browns are so rich and yummy. I figured you had a secret ingredient." The Hot Brown was a Kentucky classic, an open-faced sandwich piled with roasted turkey, bacon, and tomatoes on thick slices of hearty bread and pulled together with the creamy white sauce.

"You figured right. And I'm thinking about changing up our Hot Browns, for what it's worth."

"Why? They're so good!"

"Maybe I can make them even better." Hannah had been thinking of trying out a new spin on the local favorite. It would be a bit risky, since the dish was a longtime statewide tradition, and Hannah was well aware that messing with tradition could be a problem around there. But if she was right—and she usually was about food—her special twist would be a hit with the locals.

But that was beside the point now. She continued to think through the menu. She didn't need eggs for most of the dinner items—the Five Alarm Burger, the Flamethrowers chicken wings, the Pull Box sandwich, and the Rookie Meltdown sandwich were all big sellers so far, but none required eggs, since she bought the buns premade. But there was a new item on the menu.

"If last night was any indication, the Breakfast Burger will be a high-demand item. So I'll need eggs for that."

"I had a bite of Neil's last night. That fried egg on top is inspired."

"Glad you liked it." Hannah did a quick mental calculation based on the week's sales thus far. "Can I get twenty dozen a week?"

The question held a good amount of hesitation. Though Lacy had assured Hannah that her chickens were more productive than ever and her egg business was booming, that many eggs every week seemed like a big ask.

"Done." Lacy jotted a note in her notebook and then closed the cover with a snap. "That's no problem."

"Really? You have that many?"

"My ladies are very happy, so they produce a lot."

They talked about pricing, and even with the increased amount, the number seemed more than fair.

"More lemonade?" Lacy asked.

Hannah shook her glass gently, and the ice tinkled softly. "I wouldn't say no."

Lacy refilled both their glasses then started sorting through the stack of mail. "Why do all the bills arrive at once?"

"It always seems to happen that way, doesn't it?" The second glass of lemonade was just as good.

Lacy flipped through the mail, stopping when she came to a padded manilla envelope. She squinted at the handwriting on the front. "That's odd. It's from my mother."

"Why would she mail something to you?"

"I don't know. If she has something for me, she usually gives it to me." Flipping over the envelope, Lacy opened it and slid out a thick packet of white tissue paper. Inside was a piece of yellowed fabric, folded to form a pouch. Nestled between the folds of cloth lay a metal object.

"It's a key." Lacy picked it up and held it between them. "A heavy one."

"That's interesting." It appeared to be quite old and made of brass. The shaft was round and thick, with notched teeth on a plate attached near the end. The head was an ornate oval, carved with some kind of design. It was about the same length as Hannah's cell phone.

Lacy held it in her palm and hefted it a few times. "I wonder what it unlocks."

"Your mom didn't include a note?"

"I don't think so." Lacy set the key down and dug back through the packing material. "No note, but she wrapped it in this weird handkerchief."

Lacy spread the fabric on the table's surface, pressing out the wrinkles with both hands. Around nine inches square, the edges had been trimmed with lace. An elaborately—but crudely—embroidered *M* faced one corner.

"It's not weird. It's pretty."

"But I've never seen it before. And what's the *M* for?" Christine's last name was Johnston.

"What's your mom's maiden name?"

"Knicely, with a silent *K* at the front."

"I bet she had to spell that one a lot for people."

"Mom always jokes that she married Dad for his last name. You almost never have to tell people how to spell Johnston." Lacy stared at the handkerchief for a minute then shrugged. "She probably pulled it out of the rag bag to wrap this in."

Hannah picked up the key to inspect it more closely. It was indeed heavy, likely solid brass. Definitely old, or at least fashioned to look old, with a burnished glow. She squinted to see details in the decorative scrollwork on the key's head. "It's a mountain," she said. "Is your mom into mountains?"

"I don't know how to answer that question. Everyone likes mountains."

Hannah chuckled. "I had a friend in California who didn't like beaches because of the sand. He didn't like how it gets everywhere and everything in your home is gritty for days after you go to the beach."

"Why in the world did your friend live in Los Angeles if he didn't like the beach?"

"I don't know. My point is that some people might feel the same way about mountains for whatever reason."

"I think my mom is fine with mountains," Lacy said with a straight face.

"Does she like to hike? Or ski? Or have some particular fondness for mountains?"

"I don't think she's ever tried skiing, and I've never known her to willingly go on a hike."

Hannah tapped the scrollwork. "So why would she send you a key with a mountain on it? And for that matter, why did she mail this to you instead of coming by the farm?"

"Or giving it to me at church tomorrow." Lacy set down the handkerchief and picked up her cell phone. "I'm going to see what this is about." She put the call on speaker as it rang.

"Hi, honey." Christine's familiar voice came through the phone. "I was about to call you."

"I'm here with Hannah, Mom. You're on speaker, FYI."

"Hello, Hannah," Christine said. "How's your dad?"

"He's doing fine, Mrs. Johnston. Thank you for asking. He was at my restaurant on Thursday."

"Hannah, I've asked you not to call me that."

"Sorry, Christine. It just feels disrespectful, I guess."

Christine laughed. "We're practically family. I can assure you I prefer it when you call me by my first name."

"I'll try," Hannah promised.

"Anyway, Mom, I got your package, and I'm kind of confused."

"Hold on." A note of confusion entered Christine's voice. "What do you mean you got my package?"

"The one you sent with the key and the handkerchief inside."

"The key and handkerchief *I* sent? You sent those things to me, along with a note I can't read because much of the ink is washed away."

"What?" Lacy's face betrayed the same confusion Hannah felt. "I didn't send you a package. I got one from you."

"The envelope says this package came from you. But I'm guessing your confusion means you didn't actually send it, any more than I sent the one you got," Christine said.

"I did not," Lacy confirmed. "So who *did* send them? And what are they about?"

Christine was quiet for a moment, and then she finally said, "I have no idea. But I guess we'd better figure it out."

Fifteen minutes later, Christine arrived at the farm and walked in through the side door that led directly to the kitchen. As happy as Hannah was to see Lacy's mother, it also brought a fresh wave of grief. She wished she could call her mother and have her come over. Mom's death eight years before had left a hole in her heart, an empty place that still ached at odd times.

"Let me see your key," Christine said, dropping a padded envelope of her own on the table. She picked up the key Lacy had gotten in the mail. "This is very similar to the one I received."

Lacy opened the padded envelope addressed to Christine and slid out the handkerchief, key, and paper. She picked up the key. "You're right."

Christine held both keys in front of her face and tilted her head back to peer at them through the bottom half of her bifocals. She laid them side-by-side in the palm of her hand. "You know, with them right next to each other like this, I do see some differences."

Hannah and Lacy both leaned close.

"They must fit two different locks," Hannah said, "but they're probably connected. They have the same design."

"I have no idea what they unlock, though," Christine admitted. She had the same reddish-brown hair and hazel eyes as her daughter, though her hair was streaked with silver, and she had laugh lines around her eyes. Seeing them standing there with their heads together, it was like Hannah was looking at a picture of Lacy now and thirty years from now. "Do you?"

"No idea. Hannah thought it might have something to do with mountains."

"Well, that's a logical conclusion, I guess," Christine said. "But I don't know anything about which mountain it might be."

"So you're not anti-mountain? Hannah thought you might be." Lacy grinned.

"What are you talking about? No one is anti-mountain, Lacy." Christine peered at them. "Honestly, you girls are silly sometimes."

Despite the strangeness of the situation, Hannah felt a sudden urge to laugh. She'd seen that exact expression on Christine's face—confusion, exasperation, and barely hidden amusement—so many times growing up, and it was fun to see that they could still spark it.

"What's that paper?" Hannah asked, trying to get back on track. She gestured to the folded sheet of paper smeared with blue ink that Christine had taken out of her envelope.

"I'm not sure, honestly," Christine said. "It looks like some kind of poem or something. Or it used to be." Christine picked up the paper and unfolded it. "It got wet, though, so the ink has run."

Hannah examined the page for herself. It looked like a poem had been copied out in peacock-blue ink, but at least half of the words were obscured.

"'Long years,'" Lacy read. "Something 'cannot fill—'"

"'The absence,'" Christine read. "Some smeared words, and then, '—and years.'"

"This line ends with 'they were fire,'" Hannah said, narrowing her eyes. "That's an odd phrase."

"And this last line ends with 'and understand.'" Lacy straightened up. "That's a whole lot of nothing. What are we supposed to make of that?"

"It would no doubt make sense if we could read the whole thing," Christine said.

"I imagine it's meant as a message of some kind," Hannah said.

"Well, it might as well be in another language for as much good as it does me," Christine said.

"How did it get wet?" Lacy asked. "Did someone put it in there like that?"

"Now that would be a cruel trick," Christine said. "Let's hope no one is truly that diabolical."

Hannah picked up the padded envelope and turned it over in her hands. There was a small tear in one corner, cutting through both the yellow paper layer and the plastic bubble wrap layer underneath. "It appears the envelope was damaged in transit somehow." The whole corner of the envelope was a slightly darker yellow, and there was a wavy line that marked where the water had spread to.

"Well, that's unfortunate," Lacy said. "It's too bad we can't see the rest of it."

"It is too bad," Hannah agreed. "Can I see your handkerchief?" Maybe she could make more sense of that.

Christine slid the handkerchief across the table and Hannah picked it up. She unfolded it and saw that it had the same elegant *M* embroidered in dark blue thread. This one too looked like it had been done by an inexperienced hand, featuring various lengths of stitches, crooked positioning, and an untidy underside.

"You don't know who M is?" Hannah asked.

"Not a clue," Christine said.

"Is there any chance it's a W?" Lacy asked, rotating it.

"Don't letters usually face the corner?" Hannah asked. "It's facing the wrong way if it's a W."

"I don't see a lot of handkerchiefs these days, but that makes sense to me," Lacy replied.

"It looks old." Christine ran her fingers over the stitching.

"It would have to be," Lacy said. "Like I said, who even uses handkerchiefs anymore, let alone monogrammed ones?"

"It does hearken back to a different time, doesn't it?" Christine said. "It seems so civilized, honestly."

"Seems unsanitary to me," Lacy said with a grimace.

"In any case, I haven't seen anyone using one in my lifetime," Hannah said. She continued to study the handkerchief, running her fingers gently over the soft fabric and the lace trim. "Lacy."

Lacy turned to her. "Yes?"

Hannah indicated the lace trim. "I mean, the handkerchief is lacy. Do you think…" But she let her voice trail off. She wasn't even sure what she was getting at.

"I didn't send it, I promise you," Lacy said.

"I know that. But I was wondering whether it might be a signal of some kind." The words sounded ridiculous to Hannah even as she said them.

"Like it was meant for me?" Lacy held up the envelope. "The fact that it was addressed to me told me that already."

"I don't know." She was grasping at straws. But there had to be something here. Something to tell them who had sent these packages, and why they'd decided to make it look like Lacy and Christine had sent them to each other. "What about the handwriting? Do you recognize that?"

Both women studied the writing on the envelopes. The names and addresses had been printed with black marker in the same handwriting.

"It's different than the writing on the poem," Christine said, comparing the smeared piece of paper to her envelope. The writing was indeed different, the envelope letters all uppercase and composed with a confident hand, while the poem appeared to have been written in script by a shakier hand.

"Well, I'm stumped," Christine said. "I don't understand."

"I don't either," Lacy said. "Maybe there was supposed to be an explanation somewhere, and it got lost. Maybe it fell out through the hole in the envelope."

"Maybe," Christine said dubiously.

Hannah thought it sounded unlikely too—the hole was tiny—but didn't want to say so. "If we can't figure it out, it can't be all that important, right?"

"I suppose." Now Lacy sounded unconvinced.

They were all quiet. For a moment, the only sound was the ticking of the grandfather clock in the hallway. Then Christine said, "You repainted the pantry door."

"Yes," Lacy said, sounding as startled by the observation as Hannah felt. "I've been meaning to do it for ages, but we're slowly getting around to things, one at a time."

"You didn't like the yellow?"

"It's not that we didn't like it. It just didn't go with the colors in here anymore," Lacy said carefully.

Suddenly the air had grown tense. Hannah didn't understand why, but she decided to stay out of it.

Christine eyed the door for a moment, and then she finally nodded and said, "It looks nice. You've done a great job updating this place."

"Thanks, Mom." Lacy smiled, but her eyes remained guarded.

"Well, I should probably get going," Christine said. "I'm supposed to pick up Melba in a few minutes. She convinced me to try a water aerobics class, Lord help me." Hannah recognized the name of Christine's best friend. Because she worked as a nurse at the elementary school, Christine was off for the summer, and Lacy had said she was taking advantage of the time to try new things. "But I don't know what to do with all of this." Christine indicated the key, the handkerchief, and the poem. "It's not the kind of thing the police would investigate, is it?"

"I doubt it," Lacy said. "Not unless they turn out to be stolen or something like that. But we don't have any proof that a crime was committed."

"More likely it's some kind of joke," Christine said. "Though I don't have any clue what the point of that would be, or who would think it's funny."

"There must be a way to figure out who sent them," Hannah said. She wanted to understand what was happening here. This was too great a puzzle to simply ignore. "Would it be all right if I took a picture of them? Maybe I can figure out what's going on."

"That's fine with me," Christine said, and Lacy agreed.

Hannah dug out her phone and snapped photos of the keys, both handkerchiefs, and the smeared paper that had been in Christine's envelope. She also took pictures of the envelopes themselves, front and back.

"Thank you, Hannah." Christine gathered her package and its contents then headed for the side door. "Let us know if you figure it out."

"Tell Melba I said hi," Lacy called. Christine waved in acknowledgment left. Lacy sighed when the door closed behind her.

"What's up?" Hannah asked at once.

"Nothing. I'm sure she doesn't mean anything by it."

The mysterious tension became clear to Hannah. "The pantry door?"

Lacy nodded. "I know she spent decades cooking in this kitchen, so she still sees it as hers. She can't help it. But it almost seems like a personal affront to her every time we change something. It's a struggle to make this place feel like our own when she still feels like it's hers."

"It sounded like she was trying to be okay with it, at least," Hannah said.

"She is, but I can still tell that it bothers her. It took her a month to come to terms with it when I put new curtains on the window over the sink."

Hannah tried to choose her words carefully. "I'm sure it's hard to see changes in something that holds so many memories for her."

"I know. And it's all wrapped up with her recollections of Dad, so it's wonderful and painful all at once. I mean, they were married for almost forty years, and this house has echoes of him in every corner."

"Was it weird, having her move out so you could move in?" Hannah had still been in California when that happened, so she had missed most of it.

"It was weird. In fact, I didn't want her to go. We begged her to stay. We said she could stay in the first-floor suite, or take over the whole upstairs, or whatever she wanted. She said we'd want our space, so we offered to fix up the cottage on the east side of the property—the one she and Dad lived in when they were first married, before Grandpa passed and they took over the main house. But she didn't want to. She said it's our home now and she wanted a fresh start anyway. I must admit, I was a little annoyed. Why did she want to move out so badly? But she was insistent."

"It would be nice to have her so close."

"I thought so too. And I worry about her without Dad. But she wanted to move out, so we respect that. But that makes it annoying when she comes back and gets upset about the fact that we're making it our own. Like, wasn't that what she told us to do?"

"I'm sure she doesn't mean it that way," Hannah said. "I'm sure she wants you to be happy here."

"Yeah, probably." Lacy leaned against a countertop. "You know what would be another advantage of having her live here?"

"What?"

"This whole key thing wouldn't have happened. There wouldn't be any question of mailing things to each other," Lacy said with a smile.

Hannah couldn't help but laugh as she checked the time. "That's very true. And on that note, I'd better get going. If I don't get back soon, Jacob will revamp the menu, even though we recently updated it. He was trying to talk me into a rack of lamb yesterday."

"That does sound good, but it might be a bit too fancy for the locals." Lacy laughed. "Thank you, Hannah. Did you mean it when you said you'd try to figure out who sent these things?"

"Of course I meant it."

"Thanks. I can't help but think—well, I keep wondering if it could be something important. And I don't have the slightest clue what it's about, but I want to find out."

"Don't worry," Hannah assured her friend. "We'll figure it out together."

A Note from the Editors

We hope you enjoyed the first book in the Mysteries of Blackberry Valley series, published by Guideposts. For over seventy-five years, Guideposts, a nonprofit organization, has been driven by a vision of a world filled with hope. We aspire to be the voice of a trusted friend, a friend who makes you feel more hopeful and connected.

By making a purchase from Guideposts, you join our community in touching millions of lives, inspiring them to believe that all things are possible through faith, hope, and prayer. Your continued support allows us to provide uplifting resources to those in need. Whether through our communities, websites, apps, or publications, we inspire our audiences, bring them together, and comfort, uplift, entertain, and guide them. Visit us at guideposts.org to learn more.

We would love to hear from you. Write us at Guideposts, P.O. Box 5815, Harlan, Iowa 51593 or call us at (800) 932-2145. Did you love *Where There's Smoke*? Leave a review for this product on guideposts.org/shop. Your feedback helps others in our community find relevant products.

Find inspiration, find faith, find Guideposts.
Shop our best sellers and favorites at
guideposts.org/shop
Or scan the QR code to go directly to our Shop

More Great Mysteries Are Waiting For Readers Like *You*!

Whistle Stop Café Mysteries

"Memories of a lifetime...I loved reading this story. Could not put the book down...." —ROSE H.

Mystery and WWII historical fiction fans will love these intriguing novels where two close friends piece together clues to solve mysteries past and present. Set in the real town of Dennison, Ohio, at a historic train depot where many soldiers once set off for war, these stories are filled with faithful, relatable characters you'll love spending time with.

Mysteries & Wonders of the Bible

"I so enjoyed this book....What a great insight into the life of the women who wove the veil for the Temple." —SHIRLEYN J.

Have you ever wondered what it might have been like to live back in Bible times to experience miraculous Bible events firsthand? Then you'll LOVE the fascinating **Mysteries & Wonders of the Bible** novels! Each Scripture-inspired story whisks you back to the ancient Holy Land, where you'll accompany ordinary men and women in their search for the hidden truths behind some of the most pivotal moments in the Bible. Each volume includes insights from a respected biblical scholar to help you ponder the significance of each story to your own life.

Mysteries of Cobble Hill Farm

"Wonderful series. Great story. Spellbinding. Could not put it down once I started reading." —BONNIE C.

Escape to the charming English countryside with **Mysteries of Cobble Hill Farm**, a heartwarming series of faith-filled mysteries. Harriet Bailey relocates to Yorkshire, England, to take over her late grandfather's veterinary practice, hoping it's the fresh start she needs. As she builds a new life, Harriet uncovers modern mysteries and long-buried secrets in the village and among the rolling hills and castle ruins. Each book is an inspiring puzzle where God's gentlest messengers—the animals in her care—help Harriet save the day.

Learn More & Shop These Exciting Mysteries, Biblical Stories, & Other Uplifting Fiction at **guideposts.org/fiction**